DATE DUE

Praise for Kathy Kristof's

Investing 101

"*Investing 101* by Kathy Kristof is a reader-friendly introduction to the basics of investing and personal finance.... If I had to suggest a book on investing and personal finance to an absolute beginner, it would be *Investing 101.*"
   BookPage

"... [an] excellent primer about investing. Investors will get a clearer idea of how markets work and what you can realistically expect from your retirement funds."
   The Boston Globe

"Kristof's down-to-earth style and clear prose gives her writing a decidedly user-friendly quality.... The vast majority of us worker drones who haven't yet made complete sense of things will find *Investing 101* an easy way to get started."
   Miami Herald

"In *Investing 101,* Kathy Kristof skillfully guides the novice investor, step by step, along the path to investment success. It's an ideal primer for anyone who wants to enter the financial world and would like a helping hand."
   MYRON KANDEL
   Financial Editor, CNN

"Not only is this book more simple and straightforward than the typical book on investing, it's also more humorous and personal."
   Today's Librarian

Advance praise for Kathy Kristof's

Taming the Tuition Tiger

"Here's everything you need to know about rounding up money for higher education. For parents, it's a must-read."
> JANE BRYANT QUINN
> *Newsweek* columnist and author of *Making the Most of Your Money*

"Kathy's writing style continues to amaze me. She has a unique ability to take incredibly confusing topics and make them clear as a bell. I thought I knew a lot about options for saving for college. However, I learned new angles and opportunities on page after page of *Taming the Tuition Tiger*. If you are a parent and don't know how to tackle college costs, you will after reading this."
> CLARK HOWARD
> Syndicated radio show host
> Author of *Get Clark Smart*

"Kathy Kristof's *Taming the Tuition Tiger* is simply the best, smartest, and most comprehensive guide to financing education that I've ever read. Kristof cuts through the confusion about saving, investing, financial aid and taxes. Instead of giving generic advice, she offers specific strategies tailored to different income levels and financial situations. This book is a must-read for any parent who's concerned about paying for a child's education."
> LIZ PULLIAM WESTON
> Personal finance columnist, MSN Money
> Author of nationally syndicated "Money Talk" newspaper column

Taming the
Tuition Tiger

ALSO BY KATHY KRISTOF

Investing 101

OTHER TITLES FROM BLOOMBERG PRESS

StreetWise: A Guide for Teen Investors
by Janet Bamford

Kids and Money:
Giving Them the Savvy to Succeed Financially
by Jayne A. Pearl

The Money Making Guide to Bonds:
Straightforward Strategies for Picking the Right Bonds
and Bond Funds
by Hildy Richelson and Stan Richelson

Get in the Game!:
The Girls' Guide to Money & Investing
by Vanessa Summers

A complete list of our titles is available at
www.bloomberg.com/books

Taming the Tuition Tiger

Getting the Money to Graduate—
with 529 Plans, Scholarships,
Financial Aid, and More

Kathy Kristof

BLOOMBERG PRESS
PRINCETON

First edition published 2003
1 3 5 7 9 10 8 6 4 2

Library of Congress Cataloging-in-Publication Data

Kristof, Kathy
    Taming the tuition tiger : getting the money to graduate--with 529 plans, scholarships, financial aid, and more / Kathy Kristof. -- 1st ed.
        p. cm.
Includes index.
    ISBN 157660134-X (alk. paper)
    1. College costs--United States. 2. Tuition--United States. 3. Student aid--United States. I. Title.

LB2342 .K75 2003
378.3'8--dc21   2002155817

Acquired and edited by Kathleen A. Peterson

Book design by Barbara Diez Goldenberg

To Samantha and Michael

List of Worksheets and Charts

Acknowledgments

A JOURNALIST IS ONLY AS GOOD AS HER SOURCES. I AM infinitely grateful to mine. A wide array of experts contributed to this book by offering their time and vast expertise. A few were so indispensable that they must be mentioned by name. Jack Joyce, director of guidance services at the College Board in New York, was kind enough to read every word of this book to correct my mistakes and make suggestions aimed at making the book clearer. His encyclopedic knowledge of incredibly complex financial aid formulas was invaluable.

Mark Luscombe, principal tax analyst with CCH Inc., a Riverwoods, Illinois–based publisher of tax information; Brenda Schafer, senior tax research coordinator at the national accounting firm of H&R Block; and Philip J. Holthouse, partner at the Santa Monica accounting firm of Holthouse Carlin & Van Trigt are the three most knowledgeable and reliable tax accountants I know. Without them, the sections discussing tax breaks and phaseouts would doubtless be incomplete and riddled with error.

Joseph Hurley, a New Jersey accountant who has written extensively on 529 plans, was an invaluable source on the various pros and cons of the vast array of state-sponsored savings choices.

Kathleen Peterson, my editor at Bloomberg Press, not only suggested the idea of this book, she patiently coaxed me to complete it—almost on deadline—at a point when I was distracted by other issues.

Finally, I am forever grateful to my friends and family, who provide help and limitless support. There were many times in the past year when I thought I had finally overcommitted myself so dramatically that something important was bound to fall through the cracks. Then I'd look around and realize that my sister, my mom, or one of my close friends had quietly picked up a portion of the load. The enormity of your kindness leaves me uncharacteristically speechless. Thank you.

Anything that went right with this book is directly or indirectly the result of the fine efforts of these individuals. Anything that's missing, incorrect, or incomplete is my mistake alone.

Introduction

THERE'S A CERTAIN AMOUNT OF GALLOWS HUMOR THAT goes with having a college-bound child. One friend proudly noted that, partly thanks to her hard work sitting down to read or study with her kids every night over the years, two of her offspring had already been accepted to Stanford, and the younger three were likely to be accepted to equally prestigious (and expensive) colleges. "I could kick myself!" she said. "What was I thinking?"

Another friend noted that both the good news, and the bad news, was that his son has been accepted to Princeton. Meanwhile, my daughter tells me regularly that she plans to attend Harvard, and I'm considering putting a tape of subliminal messages under her bed, saying: "Start at a junior college. Junior colleges are great!"

Naturally, we all want what's best for our kids. Generally speaking, that means college. And a good one at that. Unfortunately, with the rapid rise in the cost of college, the goal of sending your child to a great school appears increasingly remote to many families—particularly for middle-class parents who are unlikely to win large amounts of financial aid and yet don't have the wherewithal to

1

finance five-figure tuition bills without going into life-long debt. The tragedy for many is that this appearance is deceiving.

While getting the kids through college is likely to be a challenge, both practically and financially, it is eminently possible with the right combination of aid, loans, tax breaks, work, and planning. I know this because in twenty years of reporting on personal finance issues, I've developed an extensive library of books on a variety of topics related to financing college.

The College Board and Princeton Review put out terrific annual guides on financial aid and private scholarships. Joseph Hurley has written extensively on 529 plans. And any number of annual tax guides explain the year's installment of deductions and credits for college. Together, I'm guessing college information fills more than 6,000 pages in my personal library.

That begs the question: Why write more? If there's so much available, is more needed? Unfortunately, the answer is yes. While there are great single-purpose books on private scholarships, for example, that's just one piece of the college finance puzzle. So, too, is financial aid. So, too, is saving. And tax breaks. And student employment opportunities. And maybe even a "spend-to-save" plan or two. We are all going to use some combination of these things to finance college. We parents need a guide that gives a quick overview of all the pieces because we'll have to customize our own college finance puzzle, taking into account our unique needs and resources.

That's what this book is for.

It leads you through the basics, from determining how much to save to figuring out how your savings may impact your child's future ability to obtain financial aid. It does not go into vivid detail about every private scholarship you can possibly obtain, but it will tell you where to find sources of private aid both in other reference books and on the Web. *Taming the Tuition Tiger* doesn't aim to analyze every state 529 plan, but it provides the websites where you can look at your own state's plan and where you can see how that plan is rated; and it provides tips on how to analyze whether you should stick with your state's option or go elsewhere.

The idea behind this book is to give you enough information to get started and give you the resources to know where to get more, if you need it. For some parents and college-bound kids, this book is plenty. When it's not, this book provides my best assessment of the best sources for more information on any given topic. While I can't say that assessment is unbiased—we all have preferences—it's certainly unfettered by economic incentives. I have no economic interest in any of the products or resources noted here. My affiliation with the companies is purely as a professional journalist to an information source.

That said, I'll tell you frankly that this book isn't for everyone.

If you already know you want to save through a 529 plan, and you know how much you want to save, go find a book that looks at 529 plans exclusively. If you know financial aid is all that matters, there are other books that will delve deeply into the aid process and help you structure your finances to get more aid for your child. If you need only sources for private scholarships, again, this is not the main book for you. If you do want some suggestions of good books or websites on any of those topics, flip to the resource directory in the back of this book.

Taming the Tuition Tiger: Getting the Money to Graduate—with 529 Plans, Scholarships, Financial Aid, and More is the book for you if you need a little of everything—some help figuring out how much you ought to save, where to save, how your savings might impact your tax return and your child's financial aid prospects, and some ideas of what options you have if all else has failed. It's structured for busy people. The beginning of this book sets savings goals and looks at ways to save; the middle takes on tax breaks and little-known programs that may help you; the final section focuses on aid.

If your children are young, you'll probably want to start at the beginning and keep reading until you hit the chapters on financial aid. You can skip those, however, because aid formulas are revamped every few years. If your child is ten years or more away, the facts you read here are likely to change before they apply to you.

If your children are close to college age, you may want to skim the front of the book and concentrate on the back, where you can learn about pay-as-you-go tax breaks and financial aid.

Why divvy up the book and tell people what not to read? Two reasons: First, I don't know any parents who aren't pressed for time. And second, I believe that if you can save time here, you might have a little more time to spend tossing a ball around, or going to the park, or playing a game. I write about finance so that I can take economics off the table. My personal theory is that if you do your finances right, it doesn't necessarily make you rich, it just makes you able to do things without worrying about money. That makes you calmer and gives you the freedom to spend the time you'd otherwise use to work or to worry instead doing more important things, like hanging out with your family and friends.

Enjoy.

PART ONE

Where to Begin

chapter 1

Bunk to Bonanza

E VERY PARENT HAS HEARD THE HORROR STORIES.
"By the time your toddler enrolls in college, you'll spend more on college than on buying your home," one friend tells you.

"You'll have to refinance," sighs another.

"College will cost at least $200,000," wails a third.

"You'll need to get an extra job," says your spouse. "In the coal mines." OK, that was a slight exaggeration.

But what *is* absolutely true is that college myths like these are rampant. If you believe the myths, you'll do one of two things: save way too much in all the wrong ways, or throw up your hands and not save at all. Either response is foolish.

If you save too much in dedicated college accounts, you'll end up robbing other important goals and possibly subjecting yourself to tax penalties. If you don't save at all, you'll limit your child's future options—and your own.

The truth is, college is expensive. But so was day care, summer camp, and all those clothes that your children outgrew in a nanosecond. Children are expensive. Still, we manage to feed them, clothe them, and keep a roof over their heads. In other words, the fact that college is expensive does not mean that you can't afford it—no matter how old, young, or copious your offspring. You just need to plan and act reasonably.

But to handle college costs wisely, it's important to dispel the myths that might lead you to panic or paralysis:

Myth: College will cost more than $200,000 by the time today's toddlers finish high school.

Reality: College costs vary. There's no way to predict what the actual cost will be, unless you want to be specific about the kind of college you're aiming for.

Private four-year colleges are the reason for the horror stories. A year at University of Southern California or Harvard will set you back by $35,000 to $40,000, once you include the "all-in" cost of tuition, fees, books, room, board, transportation, and other miscellaneous expenses. But if your child attends a junior college, the costs amount to pocket change by comparison.

Pasadena City College in Pasadena, California, for example, currently charges $330 annually in tuition and fees to in-state residents. Books and supplies add roughly $700 to the total. The grand total of $1,030 works out to less than $100 a month. (Compare that to what you paid for day care, with the knowledge that the kids are much more trouble as teens than they were as toddlers, and this college thing begins to sound like a bargain.)

Myth: If I save for college, I'll jeopardize my child's chances of getting student aid.

Reality: This is partly true. But it's just like saying that if you have a job, you jeopardize your chances of collecting welfare. Should you quit? The full truth is that financial aid is only partly determined by how much you have in savings. The biggest factor in how much aid you qualify for is how much you earn. Certainly, people with no savings have more need for aid. They also have more need for food stamps. More important, both they and their children have fewer options when it comes to college and everything else. If you can afford to save, even a little, do it. It will help far more than it will hurt.

Myth: If my child doesn't graduate from a good college, he won't be a success in life.
Reality: One company summarizes why this is The Big Lie—DreamWorks SKG. The SKG in the company name stands for Steven Spielberg, Jeffrey Katzenberg, and David Geffen—three multimillionaire movie moguls who started one of Hollywood's largest production companies at a time when not a single one of them had a college degree. Spielberg later went on to get his degree—a thank-you to his parents and a lesson for his kids. But when he graduated in 2001, he had nothing left to prove to the world at large. He'd already earned hundreds of millions of dollars making blockbuster and award-winning films ranging from *ET* to *Jaws* to *Schindler's List*. Did he go to a world-renowned university? You decide. Spielberg got his degree from California State University at Long Beach. Incidentally, DreamWorks is not the only major firm run by people who didn't complete college. It's just one of the more notable ones.

Smart, ambitious kids will succeed, college or no college. College makes the path easier. It boosts the average person's earning power. And it can be an extremely enjoyable way to spend four years of your life. But if your child has other dreams and the desire to pursue them, don't despair. College doesn't dictate the terms of your life. You do.

Myth: The payback for the cost of Ivy League schools is the increased earnings of their graduates.
Reality: It's the kid, not the college, who ultimately determines economic success, according to a study coauthored by Princeton economist Alan Krueger. The study tracked a group of individuals from college to twenty years later. It found that the earnings of children who were accepted by the Ivies but chose to attend non-Ivy League colleges were nearly identical to the earnings of individuals who attended the Ivies. In other words, if the Ivies offer an economic

edge, it's not a lasting one. After the first few years out in the work-force, what matters is the drive and initiative of the individual.

Myth: Community and junior colleges are glorified high schools. Students who want a good education should go to four-year schools.

Reality: "Two-year colleges are one of the best things we have going in higher education," said Terry Hartle, senior vice president of the American Council on Education in Washington, D.C. Not only is the education often comparable to the best of the four-year schools, it's usually provided at a fraction of the cost of four-year universities. "For those who want a two-year degree, they're a great way to go," said Hartle. They're also a smart option for budget-conscious kids who want to get undergraduate requirements finished before trans-ferring to a four-year university. "Notably, *roughly 40 percent* of all college students are currently enrolled in two-year community colleges," he said.

The one caveat: Students who intend to go on to graduate with a four-year degree should be sure to talk to an academic counselor to structure their class loads with an eye toward the eventual transfer. Some courses will simply not be accepted for transfer credit by certain schools, forcing the student to retake classes he or she has completed in junior college. If you take classes that won't transfer, you've not only wasted your money, you've wasted your time.

Myth: My child will qualify for academic or athletic scholar-ships, so I don't need to save.

Reality: If your child qualifies for a full-ride scholarship, congrat-ulations—and beware. Out of roughly 15 million college students, there are only a few thousand on full academic or athletic scholar-ships, experts note. Moreover, it requires a great deal of continued commitment from the student to maintain these scholarships through four years of study.

If your child suddenly decides that she no longer can stand to play soccer, for example, the scholarship evaporates. If the grades drop, so do the academic scholarship dollars. It's highly likely that you'll need to pay at least some of the costs of college, no matter how brilliant or athletic your child. Preparing now will save you a world of worry later.

Myth: Unless you're superrich, you'll qualify for financial aid.
Reality: Every family qualifies for *loans*. However, outside of a handful of merit-based scholarships, real aid—scholarships, grants, and subsidized loans—goes to families in need. Need is determined by the family's income and assets and the total cost of the college the student attends. Many middle-income families don't qualify for any aid, even if they have no savings. Many private colleges will have you refinance your home before they'll consider you a needy candidate for their scholarships.

Myth: Unless you're really poor, you won't qualify for aid. You shouldn't even bother to apply.
Reality: The determination is based not only on your income and assets, but also on the cost of the school. Many middle-income and even upper-income families can qualify for some type of aid—okay, probably loans—when their children pick pricey colleges. But, you can't even get unsubsidized student loans without filling out the financial aid forms. If there is the slightest chance that your child could qualify for aid, fill out the forms. It's worth the effort.

Myth: There are billions of dollars in scholarships that are not claimed every year.
Reality: Find one. This is a claim most often made by scholarship search services, which charge exorbitant fees to find some of this supposedly unclaimed aid for your child.

There are lots of specialized scholarships, including scholarships for left-handed tennis players and students who want to study wine making, but unless your child fits the bill, he is not going to get one. It's smart to look at your company, clubs, and trade groups and apply for any scholarship they offer—no matter how small—for which your child qualifies. After all, any dollar you're given as a gift is a dollar that you don't need to take from savings or borrow. But don't be fooled; getting these scholarships is a competitive process. Nearly every scholarship that's offered has more applicants than money. Chapter 13 offers tips on finding private scholarships and grants. However, don't fall for false promises made by search services that charge up-front fees. The Federal Trade Commission says that any service that promises a scholarship for a fee is a scam.

Myth: I can't possibly save enough, so it's foolish even to try.

Reality: Any dollar you save today provides you with more options tomorrow. Naturally, it's impossible to know if your savings will prove to be adequate until your child actually reaches college age and starts spending the stockpile. But the only thing that's foolish is not saving at all.

Just the Facts

College costs have given rise to this array of myths for two simple reasons: The average costs are high, and they're rising much faster than the rate of inflation.

The average cost of tuition and fees at a four-year public university was $4,081 in the 2002–2003 academic year, according to the College Board, a New York City–based organization that provides a host of services to the higher education industry. Room and board would add another $5,582 to the total, which adds up to just over $9,600 annually. Estimates of other incidental costs—such as the cost of flights home, clothing, phone bills, lattes, and other sundries while away at school—add roughly $3,800 more to the total, making a net cost of more than $13,000 annually.

Worse, the average cost of tuition and fees at public universities rose 9.6 percent in 2002, roughly three times the hike in the Consumer Price Index, the government's measurement of inflation in the real world, during the same time period. For anyone whose children are more than a few years away from attending college, that inflation rate can prove daunting.

Average College Costs for Undergraduates
2002–2003 Academic Year

School Type	Tuition/Fees	Room/ Board	Books/ Supplies	Other*	Total
2-year public	$1,735	†	$727	†	$2,462
2-year private	$9,890	$5,327	$766	$1,854	$17,837
4-year public	$4,081	$5,582	$786	$2,392	$12,841
4-year private	$18,273	$6,779	$807	$1,818	$27,677

* Other includes transportation and miscellaneous costs
† Sample too small to provide meaningful information

SOURCE: THE COLLEGE BOARD ANNUAL SURVEY OF COLLEGES 2002–2003

If it continues, the $13,000 average annual cost of attending a public university will rise to $51,416 within fifteen years. That would make the four-year cost $205,664.

However, that number requires context. Inflation will likely boost average salaries over that fifteen-year period, too. If inflation runs about 3 percent per year and your salary keeps pace with inflation (not counting promotions or merit increases), a person earning $50,000 today will earn $77,898 in fifteen years. A person who earns $100,000 today would earn $155,797. Those who enjoy promotions or merit raises and/or return to work once the kids are no longer at home every day may find that the actual rise in their personal income keeps pace with the college inflation rate. In other words, don't be intimidated by the inflation-adjusted figures.

Be daunted by how hard it would be to pay today's costs with cash. It's like buying a new car every year, without the benefit of a trade-in. *That's* why you want to plan ahead and save.

13

Other Fun Facts

❑ Colleges in the western portion of the United States are generally less costly than those in the East. In-state tuition at public four-year institutions averages $3,074 in the West and $5,484 in New England, for example.

❑ If your child wants to attend an out-of-state college, you might as well go private—at least as far as expenses are concerned. Why? Public universities levy a huge surcharge on out-of-state residents. The logic behind these surcharges is actually pretty clear. State income taxes pay for the bulk of the cost of providing public college education; as a result, in-state residents should be the beneficiaries.

❑ Just over 10 percent of all college students attend universities that charge $20,000 or more in tuition and fees, according to the College Board's *2002 Trends in College Pricing* report.

❑ Nearly 40 percent attend colleges that levy tuition and fees of $4,000 or less annually.

❑ About 70 percent pay tuition of less than $8,000 annually.

Why Worry?

You can pay $8,000 annually, you say? So why worry about college expenses that are decades away? The best reason is that it protects you from future upsets. If you get sick, lose your job, or face some other unexpected event that makes it impossible for you to help pay college bills when they arrive, having some savings allows you either to finance college with that extra money or to use it to buy groceries, if that's what's more important.

Moreover, while *you* may know that you are brilliant and ambitious and highly deserving of a tremendous merit raise, some bosses are not as enlightened. As a result, it's tough to predict whether your personal income will rise as fast as the college-cost inflation rate—

or the national inflation rate, for that matter. Having some savings protects you against the unlikely possibility that your boss might not value your skills as highly as you do.

And then there's the argument for compound interest. By saving even a little as early as possible, you let your money do some of the work for you. There's more on this in Chapter 6. But here's the short version: If you need $10,000 and you wait until you need it, it costs you the full $10,000. But if you need $10,000 and start saving fifteen years in advance to pay that bill, you need to save only about $30 a month, a total of just $5,400, assuming that you earn an average of 8 percent per year on your money. The other $4,600 comes from compound investment returns. That makes your job dramatically easier.

The point is, save if you can, even if you can't save a lot.

We're from the Government and We're Here to Help

It may be an old joke to some, but when it comes to financing college, Uncle Sam really is willing to help, both with paying the immediate cost of college and with helping parents save for it. This help comes in three forms: Financial aid, tax deductions and credits for those in the process of paying college bills, and tax-favored savings options for those who have time to accumulate college nest eggs.

Those with small children and plenty of time before college should know that there are more tax-favored ways to save for school than ever before. And it's not just for college. The new Coverdell education savings accounts, formerly known as education IRAs, allow parents to save tax free for private grammar school and high school expenses. The ever-popular 529 plans help high-income families sock away hundreds of thousands of dollars—enough to send a troop of Girl Scouts through college. And, assuming the money is used to finance education, whether that's college or trade school, all of the interest earned on the account is tax free.

Meanwhile, you can get tax credits for paying for college and tax deductions for paying interest on student loans. And there are special college savings programs that can match your savings for school, if you're a low-income worker willing to undergo some financial education in the process.

But, as is true with virtually anything related to government programs, there are plenty of restrictions, caveats, tricks, and traps. For instance, some of the new tax breaks for saving for school can be used together. Others are mutually exclusive. Your ability to contribute to different types of college savings accounts or to claim education deductions and credits are often affected by your income. And the income restrictions vary from tax break to tax break, account to account.

This book deals with all three types of help, as well as some strategies that aren't particularly tax related. The best strategies for you will hinge on the age of your children, how much you have to save, and your goals. Since parents of toddlers don't currently need to contemplate the vagaries of student loans—or even pay-as-you-go tax breaks—and since parents of teenagers probably aren't well served by the tax-deferred savings programs, the rest of this chapter is largely aimed at helping you skip to the sections most pertinent to your personal situation.

What's Your Scenario?

If you want to save some time, find where you fit in the sections below and then skip to the chapters that suit your scenario.

Saving for Young Children

Tax-favored savings strategies work best for those with children under the age of 12, simply because the tax breaks you receive on these accounts save your investment earnings from tax. If you save prodigiously for long periods, that can be a healthy benefit. But if you're saving for short periods—in other words, your children are 12 or older—your investment earnings are not likely to add up to much, which means these tax savings are negligible. Meanwhile, these tax-deferred accounts place loads of restrictions on how you can spend the money. The bottom line: Use tax-favored accounts only if you have enough time to enjoy the rewards. If time is short, forego the tax-deferred savings plans for other strategies that don't limit how you spend.

But, I digress. If your kids are young, you'll want to figure out how much to save each month in Chapter 2, "Setting the Stage." In addition, you'll want to learn about the three possible tax-favored accounts that can hold your money: Coverdell education savings accounts (Chapter 3); 529 plans (Chapter 4); and the old standard, Uniform Gift to Minors Act accounts (Chapter 5).

If you need help investing this dough, turn to Chapter 6. Finally, there's a loyalty spending program that may be worth considering (see Chapter 8). If you have generous relatives who are willing and able to kick in for your child's college expenses, read Chapter 9, too.

These chapters explain how much to save and provide details on the variety of tax-favored options from which you can choose.

Paying for Private Grammar School

There is just one tax-favored savings vehicle that can help you pay for private grammar school expenses. If you have kids who hope to go to a pricey high school before the pricey college, check out Chapter 3 to learn about Coverdell accounts. It's important to note that a tax law passed in the summer of 2001 made it possible to save in *both* a Coverdell account and a 529 plan (see Chapter 4) at the same time, something that wasn't previously allowed. If your education needs are likely to get costly early and stay that way—and you've got enough discretionary income today to start socking some money away—doing both is the best way to go.

Saving for Teens and Tweens

If you're getting a late start—your child is 11 or 12 and you haven't got a dime in the bank—start with Chapter 2, "Setting the Stage" and pay particular attention to the "Nontraditional Strategies" section at the end of the chapter. Read about the spendthrift's college saving plan in Chapter 8 and plan on conscripting a few relatives to help contribute to your child's college fund. Finally, if your child has a wealthy grandparent, Chapter 9 helps explain the estate tax benefits of paying college bills for your heirs.

Naturally, you can also read the chapters on tax-favored savings accounts, but realize that they are unlikely to do you much good. The benefit of these accounts is their ability to allow the investment earnings on your savings to grow on a tax-deferred or tax-free (or both) basis. But when you don't have a lot of time to build up savings and investment earnings, that's a relatively small benefit. (The discussion on pages 41–43 explains why.)

Moreover, if the money is saved in your child's name, it may jeopardize his or her ability to get a piece of the estimated $85 billion in aid available to college students. And, if you or your child should need to use the money in a tax-favored account for a purpose other than education, you can trigger onerous tax penalties. (The exception is the UGMA; see Chapter 8.) Generally speaking, for those with just a few years to go, it's not worth the risk.

That doesn't mean that parents in this situation shouldn't save—quite the contrary. But your savings should be in your own name, not in a dedicated college account. Refer to Chapter 6 for some tips on investing your money.

Coping with Imminent College Costs

Don't panic. Chapters 10, 11, 12, 13, and 14 are for you. These chapters tell you about pay-as-you-go tax breaks, financial aid, student loans, and monthly payment plans. And they dive into other ways kids can budget their college bills. It may not be perfect, but few things in life are.

Adult Students

Going back to school to boost your paltry income? Read Chapter 7 to learn about a little-known program that may provide some help. Otherwise, start at Chapter 10 and keep reading through the resource directory at the end of the book. Also, be sure to check with your current employer to see if it subsidizes education costs for workers. Many employers do, especially if you are studying a job-related subject.

High-Income Parents

Pay particular attention to Chapter 4 on 529 plans and, if you want to save for private high schools, read the "Making the Threshold" section of Chapter 9 (pages 145–146). Those who earn more than set amounts are shut out of most tax-favored savings options, but your less well-heeled relatives are not. Nothing in the tax code prevents them from helping you.

Everyone

The amount of good information on finding the right college, paying for college, getting student aid, and finding private scholarships is overwhelming. But for those who want or need more information, Chapter 15 aims to cull the clutter and direct you to what this author believes are some of the best websites, books, brochures, and information lines available.

chapter 2

Setting the Stage

PARENTS HAVE ONLY ONE PROBLEM WHEN IT COMES TO figuring out how much to save for their children's college expenses: Their children.

The best time to do this planning is when they're tiny little infants, because then you'd have plenty of time to save and have your savings generate investment earnings to help defray the often-staggering cost of education. Unfortunately, they aren't born with little stickers saying "Destined for Princeton" or "Trade school, here I come!" emblazoned on their foreheads or bums—or anywhere else, for that matter. (I know this because I turned my children over several times, looking for instructions. Not a word anywhere.)

So, as usual, we adults are left to give it our best shot, armed with virtually no information about what they'll want; what they'll qualify for; and what other resources they might have at the time, such as scholarships or grants.

How much do you need to save? Which savings vehicle is the best choice? What happens if you haven't saved enough?

How Much Is Enough?

Let's be clear: You can't possibly know how much you need to save if your child is under the age of 10. At this point, you don't know what kind of colleges your child will be interested in and what kind of schools will be interested in your child. You also don't know what will happen to college costs in the ensuing seven to eighteen years, depending on whether you're saving for an infant or a grammar schooler. Consequently, you have to make a decision about how much you want to save, given what you know about your adult family—where you went to school, how much of that cost was paid for, how you felt about college yourself, how much you can afford now, and how much you think you'll be able to afford later.

In that vein, consider whether you want to pay for all or only some of your child's education, or whether you are willing to put up a set amount—say, $10,000—that he can use for education or toward buying a home, depending on what happens down the road.

If you want to pay for all of the education, or even two years of it, you'll have to make an educated guess about what that's likely to cost.

On the High End

Today the cost of many Ivy League schools and other costly private schools amounts to between $25,000 and $40,000 per year. That cost includes tuition, fees, books, room, board, transportation, and other miscellaneous expenses that are estimated by the college. Consequently, a family wishing to prefund four years of private school would need to save between $100,000 and $160,000 per child, in today's dollars.

College-cost inflation at private schools is currently running 6 percent to 7 percent on average annually, according to the College Board. The impact of that inflation: If your child is age 7 or 8, and the current college cost inflation rate remains constant, you'll need $180,000 on the low end of the range. Instead of needing $160,000 for a private education, you'd need $315,000 for four years at Harvard or Yale.

(Notably, simply multiplying the one-year cost by four—what we did above to get the four-year cost—does not account for college-cost inflation over the four-year college enrollment period. Theoretically, to get to the proper savings number, you'd need to add $1,375 to the $25,000 first-year cost to account for an estimated 5.5 percent college-cost inflation rate in year two; then you'd have to add $1,450.63 to the $26,375 cost of year two to get the cost for year three, and so on. But to simplify the calculations, we've made the assumption that you'll save the cost for four years of education in advance. Then, presumably, the interest earned on the three years' worth of unused savings in the first year will defray the college-cost inflation rate in the second year, and so on in subsequent years.)

Mid-range

The average cost of a four-year public college or university is $12,841 annually, which includes tuition, fees, books, room, board, transportation, and "other" (read: dinner, movies, clothes, Starbucks). But the public school inflation rate is higher—about 9.6 percent today. For those with ten years to go, that raises the all-in cost in the neighborhood of $120,000. (You'll get a chance to calculate your personal inflation rate later in this chapter, using a multiplier based on the number of years your child has before she enrolls in college.)

Bargain

Those who want an education at a bargain price could start at a junior or community college, where the costs are equivalent to the cost of sending your preteen to summer camp. A two-year public school will set you back an average of $2,400 annually for tuition, books, and fees. This can be an excellent and cost-effective option for those pursuing careers that require only two-year degrees. Those who aren't averse to the idea of completing two years of general-education requirements at a community college before they transfer to a four-year school can save a small fortune on education. Better yet, students who have successfully completed two years at a community college have a far greater chance of getting into a college with highly selective admissions criteria, college experts maintain. There are several reasons why—including the fact that a child who has completed two years of college and wants to continue is more likely to graduate with a four-year degree than a high school senior, and colleges are rated on their graduation statistics. In any event, it's not time wasted.

Meanwhile, this strategy would save the individual who wanted to graduate from an Ivy League or other highly selective private school $45,000 to $75,000 in today's dollars, and it would save the public school aspirant about $20,000. If your child needs a little inspiration, you might want to remind her that the difference equates to a down payment on a house. That's something you certainly won't be able to afford to help with if you've already put yourself in the poor house paying for college. Or, tell your child you're not paying for school. That might make the child highly budget-conscious in a hurry.

Specific School Costs

An indispensable tool available to those seeking specifics on particular colleges and universities, where you can get any school's current-year costs, resides at www.collegeboard.com. This wonderful website allows you to type in the name of a school in a box on the left-hand side of the home page. The site responds with a laundry list of information, including the address, admission information, financial aid policies, and current costs of the school.

Formulate a Plan

Armed with preliminary information on the costs associated with the type of college you anticipate for your child, you can begin to formulate a plan, whether you're banking on a particular school or a particular type of school. Consider what you want for your child. Do you want him to feel that he has earned this education by paying for all or a portion of it? If so, you may want to save only for extras—perhaps room and board, transportation home during breaks, a computer, or even just books or food. Or perhaps you'll want to save for the estimated tuition costs, but have your child pay for all the extras.

If, on the other hand, you want your child to concentrate solely on studies and never worry about the cost of schooling, your savings goals will be greater. You'll want to set aside a substantial amount of the all-in cost in advance.

Naturally, if your child is old enough to be a part of this decision, your savings strategy should incorporate her wants, needs, and abilities. A child who has the ability to work and save for school may well be able to help finance his or her own education. Not only will this take some of the pressure off you, it may make the education more valuable to that child.

It's worth noting that college costs do not need to be paid in advance. You may have the ability to pay some or even all of the costs as you go along, if you prefer. Although saving part of the tab in advance is recommended—it simply gives you more options and flexibility later, and it cuts down on the risk of having some economic upset derail your child's plans—if your personal circumstances make pay-as-you-go much more affordable than advance savings, look to Chapter 14 for information about how to set up monthly payment plans.

Those who want to save at least something now need to use this information to determine a reasonable savings goal. You can arrive at a rough number by filling out the worksheet that follows with information about your child and the cost of the specific university or type of college that you expect him to attend. Then use the mul-

---

WORKSHEET

College Cost Calculator

1 Child's name:_____

2 Child's age: _____

3 Number of years to college: _____

4 Aspiration (public/private/two-year/four-year education):

_____

5 Estimated annual cost*: $_____

6 Number of years in college: _____

7 Rough need in current dollars (multiply line 5 by line 6):

$_____

8 Estimated college-cost inflation rate (a reasonable guesstimate would range between 5 percent and 8 percent annually):_____

9 Multiplier (use the chart at right to match the number of years before your child enrolls in college with the estimated inflation rate you expect for the cost of education):   _____

10 Goal (multiply the figure on line 7 by the multiplier on line 9. This tells you roughly how much you'll need to have on hand, if you wish to prefund all college bills.): $_____

*See Average College Costs for Undergraduates on page 13 or go to www.collegeboard.com.

tipliers in the College-Cost Inflation table to roughly estimate the tab when your child is ready for higher education.

Estimating College-Cost Inflation

Use the multipliers in the chart at right to figure roughly what your need in today's dollars translates into when your child actually enrolls in college. To find the right multiplier, match the number of years you have until he or she enrolls to the inflation rate that you anticipate. Currently, tuition and fees are rising by about 6 percent at private, four-year universities and rising by more than 9 percent at four-year

College-Cost Inflation					
Time to Goal			Anticipated Inflation Rate		
	4%	5%	6%	7%	8%
3 years	1.125	1.158	1.191	1.225	1.260
4 years	1.170	1.215	1.262	1.311	1.360
5 years	1.216	1.276	1.338	1.402	1.469
6 years	1.265	1.340	1.418	1.501	1.587
7 years	1.316	1.407	1.504	1.606	1.714
8 years	1.368	1.477	1.594	1.718	1.851
9 years	1.423	1.551	1.689	1.838	1.999
10 years	1.480	1.629	1.791	1.967	2.159
11 years	1.529	1.710	1.898	2.105	2.332
12 years	1.601	1.796	2.012	2.252	2.518
13 years	1.665	1.886	2.133	2.410	2.720
14 years	1.732	1.980	2.261	2.578	2.937
15 years	1.801	2.079	2.396	2.759	3.172
16 years	1.873	2.183	2.540	2.952	3.426
17 years	1.949	2.292	2.693	3.159	3.700
18 years	2.026	2.407	2.854	3.380	3.996

public schools. However, if you're accounting for the cost of books, board, transportation, and other miscellaneous expenses in your calculation, realize that those costs are likely to rise at the somewhat lower national inflation rate, which averages about 3 percent.

Set a Goal

Now that you've completed the College Cost Calculator worksheet, you have a better idea of what it would cost to foot the entire bill. Given what you know about the likely future cost, decide whether you want to bank $5,000, $10,000, $100,000—or more—for this future expense.

To determine this, look at how far your current savings will take you by using the Future Value of Present Savings chart on pages 30–31. For example, a family aiming for a $10,000 stockpile in five years would find that their current savings of $5,000 will be worth $6,415 based on a 5 percent annual rate of return. (That's the $5,000 multiplied by 1.283—the multiplier on page 30 for five years at 5 percent.) This family needs just $3,585 more to reach their goal. You have no savings yet? Either way, you'll need to skip to the Monthly Savings Calculator worksheet on page 29 to estimate how much you need to save today to have that amount in the future. (More on computing this below.)

Understand that all calculations require certain assumptions: that you'll save consistently, you'll earn a set return on your money, and your child will go to college in the time frame that you specify. Bear in mind that none of these assumptions is certain to remain the same.

Your circumstances may change, and you may find that you can save much more—or much less—than what's calculated here. Meanwhile, the investments you choose for the college dough could either take off or plunge in value. Your child could become a National Merit Scholar and receive so much scholarship aid that your savings are unnecessary. (Or he could become a tradesperson and not need higher education.)

My point? Don't let this be a one-time calculation. Life is fluid. Children are mercurial. Check back, now and again, on what you've done and why. Make sure that what you set up when your child was a toddler still makes sense when he or she is a "tween." If it does, great. If not, adjust.

Reaching Your Savings Goal

Record the amount you want to have saved for your child and the number of years you have until that child enrolls in school on the Monthly Savings Goal Calculator worksheet at right. To make things simple, these calculations assume that you'll have the entire college stockpile ready and waiting when your child reaches college age. But understand that your child will, or course, not need the entire amount in the first year.

WORKSHEET

Monthly Savings Goal Calculator

1 Savings goal for child: $_____

2 Number of years to college: _____

3 Amount already saved: $_____

4 Future value of current savings (multiply the figure on line 3 by the appropriate multiplier in the chart on pages 30–31): $_____

5 Additional need (subtract line 4 from line 1): $_____

6 Monthly savings required (multiply the result on line 5 by the appropriate multiplier in the chart on pages 32–33): $_____

Ideally, your child will need to drain just one-quarter—or, if you're really lucky, less—of the account each year. The remainder will remain saved, and with luck, will generate enough investment return to handle tuition inflation for subsequent years of college.

The family with a $3,585 need in five years, for instance, will match their estimated return—5 percent—and their time frame—five years—to find the appropriate multiplier—0.0147 in the Monthly Savings Per Anticipated Return Rate chart on pages 32–33. Their need of $3,585 multiplied times 0.0147 tells them they'll need to save $52.69 per month to reach their goal.

A family with a greater need—say $100,000—and more time, may decide to invest more aggressively. Over a ten-year period, they may decide an 8 percent average return is likely. They'd use the 0.0055 multiplier (from pages 32–33) to determine their monthly savings goal of $550.00.

Savings Strategies

As mentioned in the previous chapter, if you are a high-income parent planning to save a large amount for each child's college bills, you'd be wise to take advantage of one or more of the tax-favored savings vehicles now provided in the U.S. tax laws.

Future Value of Present Savings
Time to Goal

	3%	4%	5%
3 years	1.094	1.127	1.161
4 years	1.127	1.173	1.221
5 years	1.162	1.221	1.283
6 years	1.196	1.271	1.349
7 years	1.233	1.322	1.418
8 years	1.271	1.376	1.490
9 years	1.309	1.432	1.567
10 years	1.349	1.491	1.647
11 years	1.390	1.551	1.731
12 years	1.433	1.615	1.820
13 years	1.476	1.681	1.913
14 years	1.521	1.749	2.011
15 years	1.567	1.820	2.114
16 years	1.615	1.894	2.222
17 years	1.664	1.972	2.335

The best savings vehicle may, in fact, choose you rather than the other way around. If you earn more than $110,000 when single or $220,000 when married, filing a joint tax return, the only tax-deferred college savings accounts available to you are the so-called 529 plans. While these are the most complex to explain, because there are more than fifty different variations sponsored by fifty different states, they are also a great option for well-heeled parents (or other relatives) who want to maintain some control over their money. Unlike most other types of college savings accounts, the money placed in a 529 plan remains the asset of the contributor, not the beneficiary, until the money is tapped for school. That eliminates the worry that a child will use his college fund to go to Europe instead of Harvard. For detailed information on 529 plans, skip to Chapter 4.

If you earn less than those income thresholds, you may want to consider a Coverdell account for at least a portion of your savings.

		Estimated Rate of Return		
6%	**7%**	**8%**	**9%**	**10%**
1.197	1.233	1.270	1.309	1.348
1.270	1.322	1.376	1.431	1.489
1.349	1.418	1.490	1.566	1.645
1.432	1.520	1.613	1.712	1.818
1.520	1.630	1.747	1.873	2.007
1.614	1.748	1.892	2.049	2.218
1.714	1.874	2.049	2.241	2.450
1.819	2.010	2.220	2.451	2.707
1.932	2.155	2.404	2.681	2.990
2.051	2.311	2.603	2.933	3.304
2.177	2.478	2.819	3.208	3.649
2.311	2.657	3.053	3.509	4.032
2.454	2.849	3.307	3.838	4.454
2.605	3.055	3.581	4.198	4.920
2.766	3.276	3.879	4.592	5.435

Why? Coverdell accounts can be tapped for grammar as well as high school expenses. For those who think they may want to send their child to a costly private high school, or pay tutors to help him boost his grades and get into the college of his choice, this can be a great way to finance those costs. For information on precisely which education bills can be paid with a Coverdell account, as well as their other benefits and detriments, see Chapter 3.

Nontraditional Strategies

If your income is more modest, you may want to consider some less traditional ways to finance college. Why? In two words: financial aid.

As college costs have soared, so, too, has the amount that federal and

Monthly Savings Per Anticipated Return Rate

MATCH THE NUMBER of years you have to save with the average annual rate of return you expect to earn on your invested cash.
Remember that the less time you have, the less risk you should take
with your investments; thus, the less return you should expect to earn.

Time to Goal

	3%	4%	5%
3 years	.0266	.0262	.0258
4 years	.0196	.0192	.0188
5 years	.0155	.0151	.0147
6 years	.0127	.0123	.0119
7 years	.0107	.0103	.0100
8 years	.0092	.0088	.0085
9 years	.0081	.0077	.0073
10 years	.0071	.0068	.0064
11 years	.0064	.0060	.0057
12 years	.0058	.0054	.0051
13 years	.0052	.0049	.0046
14 years	.0048	.0044	.0041
15 years	.0044	.0041	.0037
16 years	.0041	.0037	.0034
17 years	.0038	.0034	.0031

state governments have made available to help lower- and moderate-
income students pay the bills. If you think you may qualify for some
of this aid, it's wise to structure your savings in a manner that won't
diminish your chances. Money saved in your child's name definitely
diminishes your ability to qualify for aid. So does money saved in your
name in a taxable account, but to a lesser degree.

Chapter 11 goes into financial aid details, which are not listed
here. However, when considering savings strategies, it's worth mentioning that what currently *does not count* in federal financial aid

		Estimated Rate of Return		
6%	**7%**	**8%**	**9%**	**10%**
.0254	.0250	.0247	.0243	.0239
.0184	.0181	.0177	.0174	.0170
.0143	.0140	.0136	.0133	.0129
.0116	.0112	.0109	.0105	.0102
.0096	.0092	.0089	.0086	.0083
.0081	.0078	.0075	.0071	.0068
.0070	.0067	.0063	.0060	.0057
.0061	.0058	.0055	.0052	.0049
.0054	.0050	.0047	.0045	.0042
.0048	.0044	.0041	.0039	.0036
.0042	.0039	.0037	.0034	.0031
.0038	.0035	.0032	.0030	.0027
.0034	.0031	.0029	.0026	.0024
.0031	.0028	.0026	.0023	.0021
.0028	.0026	.0023	.0021	.0019

formulas are dollars saved in the parents' retirement accounts and home equity. (If your child goes to a private college, the school may use a different formula. But for all publicly financed colleges, the federal formula must apply.)

As a result, those who have limited resources should seriously consider looking at the size of their mortgage and the amount they're contributing to retirement accounts before they begin flipping money into accounts dedicated to college. Paying extra against the home loan or saving more in your own retirement account can save you thousands of dollars, improve your overall financial picture, and make it easier to finance the college bill, no matter how great the cost.

The House Account

Consider how it works for a family with a $200,000, 30-year mortgage at a 7 percent fixed rate. The monthly payment on this loan would amount to $1,331. The parents have enough to pay an additional $669 monthly either into the mortgage or into college funds for their two toddlers, ages 1 and 3.

If they put the $669 into their mortgage rather than a college savings account, they would pay off the loan in 150 months—roughly 12.5 years—instead of 360 months. That would save them $178,160 in interest. It would also alleviate their household's biggest monthly expense. The result: By the time their elder child is 16, they would have $2,000 per month in additional monthly spending power—the amount they're no longer paying against the home loan. That could allow them to pay $24,000 annually toward college bills with cash.

The other benefit to this strategy is family flexibility. If it turns out that this family's children don't want to go to college, but want to start a business or get married instead, the parents can kick in money to that goal if they wish, depending on whether they consider the shift good news or bad.

If they had saved in dedicated college savings accounts—or in so-called UGMA or UTMA (see Chapter 5) accounts—the money saved would have to pay for college or go to the child, no matter what the purpose.

But doesn't paying down the mortgage mean this family will lose the tax deductions it gets for paying mortgage interest expenses? Yes. By not having to pay $178,160 in interest, this family will lose tax deductions that are probably worth roughly 30 percent of that amount, or about $53,000. They still end up about $124,000 ahead.

The 401(k) Account

An even better option for those who are not already making maximum contributions to retirement accounts may be to boost contributions to the parents' 401(k)s. Contributions to these tax-favored savings accounts come out of gross income before the tax is computed, making the out-of-pocket costs comparatively low. Most plans also allow participants to borrow up to 50 percent of the account value or $50,000, whichever is less.

Thanks to the tax law passed in 2001, maximum contribution limits to 401(k) accounts rose to $11,000 in 2002 and jumped to $12,000 annually in 2003. But the typical participant contributes about half that amount. What would happen to this hypothetical family if the parents dedicated their $669 to their 401(k)s rather than to college accounts?

Presumably, each parent would save an extra $335 monthly. That would reduce their monthly paychecks by about $234.50, assuming they're in the 30 percent federal income tax bracket. (Because 401(k) contributions are pre-tax contributions, they reduce your out-of-pocket costs by about 30 percent less than the amount you contributed, assuming you'd otherwise pay about 30 percent in federal and state income taxes on the saved income.)

By the time the first child hits college age, about fourteen years hence in our example, the parents have roughly $100,000 more in *each* retirement account than they would have had if they'd left their contribution levels alone. (That calculation assumes they earn between 7 percent and 8 percent on their money.) At that point, one parent could borrow $50,000 from the account to finance the first child's college bills. That parent would need to repay the loan, though, which would mean his monthly contributions would be higher.

As a consequence, the other parent may opt to stop contributing extra dollars so they'll have enough family income to make the additional payments to the drained 401(k). Or the parent who took out the loan could simply stop making new contributions to his own plan while the loan was being paid off. The second parent could hold her extra 401(k) dollars in abeyance, to handle child number two's college costs.

What if the kids don't go to college? Then the parents have a richer or earlier retirement.

In other words, no matter what happens, the family benefits.

PART TWO

The Skinny on
Saving, Investing, and
Tax Incentives

chapter 3

Coverdell Education Savings Accounts

C OVERDELL EDUCATION SAVINGS ACCOUNTS USED TO BE called education IRAs—a silly name, considering that IRA is an abbreviation for individual retirement account, and these accounts are not for retirement. However, when the tax laws were revamped in the summer of 2001, these accounts were revised and renamed, and they're now more attractive and flexible than ever before.

The reasons: Contributions to these accounts were once limited to $500 per beneficiary per year, but the new contribution limit is $2,000 per beneficiary per year. In addition, savings in these accounts can be used for elementary and high school costs, as well as for school supplies, computers, Internet access, and the expenses related to helping a special-needs child through school.

As long as withdrawals are made for "eligible expenses," both the principal and interest coming out of the accounts are federal tax free. (It's generally tax free on state returns, too. But not all state tax codes are consistent with federal law in this regard, so this is a point worth checking with your state tax authorities.)

Coverdell Education Savings Accounts

Maximum contribution —$2,000 annually.

Tax benefits —No up-front deductions, but the money accumulates on a tax-deferred basis.

—Withdrawals used to pay education expenses are federal income tax free.

Limitations — Contributions may be made only for a beneficiary who is under 18 years of age.

—Married couples earning more than $190,000 (jointly) annually and singles earning $95,000 or more face contribution restrictions.

—Married couples earning more than a total of $220,000 annually and for singles earning more than $110,000 are unable to contribute.

—Coverdell money must be used within thirty days of the beneficiary's thirtieth birthday or the account is considered "distributed" to the beneficiary, which will trigger tax and penalties.

Pros — Coverdell accounts can be used for elementary and secondary school expenses, as well as for college.

—They allow investment flexibility, a particular plus for those who like to manage their own savings.

Cons — Education savings accounts are counted as the child's asset when calculating eligibility for student aid.

Tricks — Contributions to these accounts can be made until April 15 of the following year.

Traps — If the money is pulled out for some purpose other than education, the investment earnings will be taxable and the taxpayer will be subject to a 10 percent penalty on the taxable portion of the withdrawal.

—A Coverdell account cannot be pledged as security for a loan. If it is, it loses its tax-exempt status.

Practical Details

Setting up a Coverdell account is very much like setting up a self-directed individual retirement account. These accounts are offered by most financial institutions, such as banks, brokers, mutual-fund companies, and even credit unions.

You get to decide which type of institution to use and how you'd like to invest the money. As with a self-directed IRA, you can invest Coverdell savings in safe (but dull and low-yielding) investments, such as money-market savings accounts, certificates of deposit, and even passbook accounts; in risky, volatile securities such as growth stocks and junk bonds; or in a mixture of things safe, risky, and moderate.

However, as with many of the new tax-favored college savings accounts, parents need to realize that the tax breaks they're getting—which is the whole reason to save in this type of account versus a basic brokerage or bank account—are solely on the investment income earned in the account. The less investment income you earn, the less valuable the tax break.

Contributions to these accounts are *not* deductible on federal tax returns. The tax breaks simply allow the investment income earned on the account to grow on a tax-deferred basis. That investment income, if used for education, will be tax free when withdrawn, too. But unless parents save big and early, the tax breaks sound better in theory than they are in practice. Let's look at a few hypothetical examples to illustrate why.

Middle-Income Parents

Bob and Robin Wright have two children, Tom, age 7, and Brittany, age 9. They open Coverdell accounts for both children, to which they will contribute $50 a month, or $600 per year, for each child. That's a total of $1,200 annually, which is about all the Wrights can afford.

41

We'll assume that half of the money is invested in bonds, earning 5 percent; the other half is invested in stocks, which appreciate by 8 percent on average annually. Bond income is normally taxable as it is received; the appreciation on the stock portfolio is generally not taxable until the shares are sold and the taxpayer has a realized gain.

We'll assume that the children's stock is in an index mutual fund, and the parents will not trade the shares until the children are ready to go to college. This means the stock investments would throw off a negligible amount of currently taxable income, regardless of whether they are in tax-deferred savings (such as a Coverdell account) or in a taxable account (such as a Uniform Gift to Minors account).

When Brittany turns 18, she will have $7,336.82 in her college coffers, of which $5,400 is principal—the contributions her parents made, which would not be taxable under any circumstances—and $1,936.82 in interest and investment earnings.

When Tom turns 18 two years later, he will have $9,652.15, of which $6,600 is principal and $3,052.15 is interest and investment earnings.

Because both children are using all that money to finance their college bills, none of it is taxable. But to assess how great a benefit that might be, you'd have to compare how much tax they would have paid if the money had been in a similar account that requires you to pay taxes as you go. The most similar vehicle is the Uniform Gift to Minors Act account, often called UGMA accounts for short. (More on these in Chapter 5.)

So how much tax would they have paid on the investment earnings accumulated in an UGMA account? Zero. Zip. Nada.

Why? In the first year, each child's account would have generated a $6.97 taxable gain from the bond investments. But each child gets a personal exemption deduction on his or her federal income tax return. The child's exemption amount is indexed for inflation, but it's currently $750 annually, which would have more than covered the tax obligation on the negligible earnings they received while their accounts were growing.

When the children cashed out of their stock investments, they would each be over the age of 14, which qualifies them for a larger personal exemption deduction. Again, that deduction would easily have covered the taxable income on the account.

What if they'd earned a better return on their money? Given the amount of money saved and the amount of time for which it was invested, it would be highly unlikely—regardless of the investment mix or optimistic assumptions about the parents' investing prowess—that the Wright children would owe any taxes. Chances are exceptionally good that no matter how this money was invested, it would never generate enough taxable income for either child to pay tax on the proceeds.

Net tax benefit of the Coverdell account over an UGMA account: $0.

It's important to note, too, that a Coverdell account puts more restrictions on the use of the child's money than does an UGMA account. UGMA dollars can be used for anything that's in the child's interest—for example, to pay for school, or to buy the child a car or clothes, or pay for his housing.

While some don't like the fact that UGMA dollars become the child's unrestricted property at the age of majority—either 18 or 21, depending on state law—there is also no restriction on how quickly or slowly the money must be spent. Theoretically, the child could accumulate assets until he or she was ready to buy a home or retire, which provides lots of flexibility. However, note that at some point, the financial institution where the UGMA account is set up may require that the account be converted from a custodial account to an ordinary taxable account. There are two reasons: First, once the child reaches the age of majority, he or she no longer needs a custodian to manage the assets (theoretically, anyway). Second, many financial institutions give kids a break on the fees and charges they impose on savings and investment accounts. Once the child is an adult, the financial institution wants to start charging adult rates.

Coverdell accounts, on the other hand, must be tapped for education, tutoring, or educational supplies before the child reaches the age of 30. If the money is used for any other purpose, the investment income becomes taxable at the child's rate. In addition, the taxable portion of the withdrawal is subject to a 10 percent tax penalty.

In this case, if Brittany suddenly decided to run off with her boy-friend and use the Coverdell savings to get married, she'd pay roughly $312.36 in federal income taxes and penalties—about 16 percent of the investment income earned in her account. (That assumes she had virtually no other income and thus was in the lowest federal income tax bracket.) That's $312 more than she would have paid in tax if the money were in an UGMA account.

If there's a fair chance that a child is not going to use the money for education, and you'd be supportive enough of that change that you wouldn't want him or her to be penalized for it by tax authorities, skip tax-favored accounts unless you are saving large amounts. The tax benefits are simply not worth the loss of flexibility.

High-Income, Big Savers

That tradeoff doesn't mean that Coverdell accounts are a bust. Some high-income families who save early and big could see a substantial benefit with Coverdell savings, especially if they're lucky enough to earn a high return on their money. Consider another hypothetical family, Sandy and Sue Stanwick and their children, toddler Tami, two years old, and newborn Todd. The Stanwicks, who are always flush with cash, put $2,000 in each child's Coverdell account each January 1. Since they can afford to make up for investment losses, if necessary, they invest aggressively and are able to earn an average of 10 percent on their children's money.

Assuming all of the money is in growth stocks, not generating any taxable earnings while accumulating, and that the Stanwicks do not trade as they go along, Tami's account is worth a tidy $71,899.50 when she's 18 and ready to enroll in college. Thirty-two thousand of that total is principal; $39,899.50 is investment income.

At a minimum, assuming that she is able to remain in the lowest tax bracket when withdrawing her money, the Coverdell account saves Tami about $3,000 in federal capital gains taxes. (That's the type of tax she'd pay if the money were in a taxable account, rather than a tax-favored account. Capital gains taxes are assessed at a 10 percent rate for those who are in the federal government's 10 percent and 15 percent marginal income tax brackets.)

Two years later, Todd's account is worth $91,198, of which $36,000 is principal and $55,198 is investment earnings. Assuming Todd uses all of that savings for school, using the Coverdell account would save him at least $5,000—and more likely twice that amount—in federal capital gains taxes. But, again, if either of these children spends the money on anything other than education, they get creamed by Uncle Sam.

Specifically, if Todd decides to tap his $91,198 to buy a Porsche, he'll owe roughly $12,675 in income taxes (this assumes a 25 percent ordinary income tax rate), plus a penalty of $5,519, for a total of $18,194 in federal income taxes and penalties. Naturally, that's considerably more than he saved by using the Coverdell account.

The Trader and the Coverdell

Coverdell accounts are a lifesaver for parents who can't help but trade securities. Those who like to actively buy and sell stocks get much greater tax benefits out of a Coverdell account, because they're not paying taxes on the taxable gains and losses they might be sustaining each year.

Active trading—buying and selling numerous securities in any given year—is a foolish way to invest. It makes good money for your broker, but it's been proven time and again to give you substandard returns. There's more on why in Chapter 6. Nonetheless, some people can't help themselves. Active trading is their form of amusement. It keeps them out of bars and gambling establishments. If this is you, a Coverdell account should be your investment vehicle of choice. You get nearly unlimited investment options and the ability to avoid capital gains taxes on any trading profits you might recognize along the way.

No other college savings vehicle gives you the combination of myriad investment choices and tax deferral. The UGMA account provides as many investment choices, but not the ability to defer tax on the gains. The 529 (see Chapter 4) allows tax-deferral (or tax-free) treatment of the gains, but your investment choices are limited, just as they are in a 401(k) plan. So for the actively trading parent, Coverdell is the account for you.

Saving for High School

Coverdell accounts are also good for high-income parents who expect to send their children to pricey private high schools.

Let's take another look at the Stanwicks to see why. They save $2,000 a year from the time each child is born. We'll also assume they're fortunate enough to earn 10 percent annually, on average, on that money. When Tami is 13 and about to enroll in prestigious Sacred Heart Academy, she has $49,045, of which $26,000 is principal and $23,045 is investment earnings. If she takes $12,000 per year to pay for tuition, fees, books, and other expenses, all of the money is tax-free.

If her parents were paying tax on the savings, it would likely cost them more than $4,600 in federal income tax, not to mention state income taxes, where applicable. If the money had been saved in Tami's name in an UGMA account, the tax hit would depend on how old she was when she withdrew the savings. Assuming she was still age 13 when paying tuition for her first year at Sacred Heart, she'd pay tax on roughly $4,900 of the $12,000 she tapped each year. That would cost her—or her parents, who are likely paying the bills—roughly $1,000, assuming that they're paying tax at a 20 percent capital gains rate. The following year, when she's taxed as an adult, she'd pay tax on only about $1,140 of the $12,000 she pulls out of savings. Assuming she gets a 10 percent capital-gains rate, that costs $114.

In the long run, the Stanwicks save a tidy sum by putting the high school money in Tami's name, and in this case, the Coverdell account saves the most.

Eligible Uses for Coverdell Savings

The Coverdell account is the only tax-deferred school savings vehicle that can be used for elementary and high school expenses. The increasingly popular 529 plan (see Chapter 4), can be used only for college and graduate school costs.

Eligible—that is, tax-free—uses for Coverdell savings are to pay for tuition, fees, books, supplies, and equipment required for enrollment or attendance in an eligible college, graduate school, vocational or trade school, or for an elementary or secondary school. Schools may be public, private, or religious. For room and board expenses to be paid with tax-fee dollars, the student must be enrolled in a degree or certificate program and be attending school at least half time. (That's defined as at least one-half of the normal full-time workload for the course of study pursued. In other words, if full-time status is bestowed on those with eighteen units, you'd have to take nine or more units to claim tax-free withdrawals from Coverdell savings to pay your room and board expenses. There's no similar restriction on withdrawals for tuition, fees, or books.)

In addition, tax-free withdrawals can be used to cover tutoring, the purchase of computers, Internet access, room, board, uniforms, and extended day-program fees for elementary and high school students.

Other Considerations

Age Restrictions

You cannot contribute to a Coverdell account for a beneficiary who is age 18 or older. The accounts must be drained—tapped, presumably to pay education expenses—within thirty days of the beneficiary's thirtieth birthday (or within thirty days following the death of a beneficiary). If the account isn't used by that point, the government will consider it "distributed" for tax purposes, which will trigger income tax and penalties.

The one exception: Special-needs beneficiaries may maintain Coverdell savings indefinitely to pay for a wide array of services, both educational and practical. The tax code doesn't specifically define special-needs child. In this case it's up to the parents to determine whether their child qualifies.

Rollover

If the intended beneficiary does not need the money for education, she may roll the money into another Coverdell account for the benefit of another member of her family. Like rollovers of individual retirement accounts, the money will be considered distributed and taxable to the beneficiary, unless it is rolled into a new account within sixty days of leaving the original account.

Eligible beneficiaries for a Coverdell rollover would include the original child's child, step-child, sister, brother, or step-sibling. Technically, it could also be a parent or step-parent or any relative of the beneficiary's parents, such as a niece or nephew. It could also be an in-law or the spouse of an in-law.

Taxable Distributions

If Coverdell assets are used for anything other than the eligible expenses listed above, the investment income becomes taxable at the recipient's ordinary income tax rate, and the taxable portion of the distribution is subject to a 10 percent excise tax.

Simply put, if the recipient is in a 10 percent income tax bracket, he or she will pay 20 percent tax on the Coverdell gains. If he is in the 25 percent bracket, the tax will amount to 35 percent of the gain.

The 10 percent penalty is waived, however, in the event of the death or disability of the beneficiary. It is also waived for funds not used for education solely as the result of receiving a scholarship. In other words, if your child receives a $10,000 scholarship, she can pull out as much as $10,000 from the Coverdell account and use it for any purpose, and she will not have to pay the 10 percent penalty on that amount. The investment earnings on the distribution will be taxable. But the penalty will not apply to the amount that corresponds with the value of the scholarship.

Financial Aid Implications

In addition to the tax hit that faces anyone who misuses Coverdell savings, there's another potentially costly shortcoming for lower- and middle-income parents who might be tempted to use these accounts. In a nutshell, Coverdell money is counted as your child's asset for student aid purposes. What that means is that federal aid authorities expect your child to spend every dollar saved in this account over the course of paying for four years of college. That will boost the "expected family contribution" amount and reduce the child's eligibility for student aid. (See Chapter 11, for more detail on how this works.)

For wealthy families, this shouldn't be a concern because the probability of qualifying for student aid is low, anyway. But it is a consideration for middle-income families like the hypothetical Wrights. Simply put, because the $7,336.82 is in Brittany's name, aid formulas figure that roughly one-third of that amount can be tapped for school expenses in any given year. If the same amount were in her parents' names, the formula would figure that only about 5 percent would be available to pay for her college bills. The bottom line: In Mom and Dad's names, the $7,336.82 reduces the family's eligibility for aid by about $367 annually. In Brittany's name, it reduces the family's eligibility by about $2,400 annually.

Coverdell Compared to Simply Saving

The aid issue begs the question: How would the Coverdell—or an UGMA account, for that matter—compare with simply saving in the parent's names in a taxable account?

During the accumulation phase, the Wrights would pay a total of $210 in income taxes on the interest earned on Brittany's bond portfolio. (We've assumed the Wrights pay a 30 percent marginal rate.) When they cash out the stocks, with a $1,235 profit, they'd pay 20 percent capital gains taxes—roughly $247 total. Together, they saved about $450 in income and capital gains taxes by saving in Brittany's name.

Because saving in Brittany's name costs them considerably more in aid eligibility, for this family, simply saving more money in the parents' bank or brokerage accounts may have been a better choice. It wouldn't have cost them a lot in federal income tax, and it leaves them with more flexibility. (They might also consider saving in so-called 529 plans, discussed in the next chapter). These plans are slightly more restrictive about the use of tax-free distributions, but under current financial aid formulas, the assets in these accounts are treated as if owned by the donor, not the child.)

To Coverdell or Not to Coverdell

How do you decide whether a Coverdell account is the best way for you to save? First, toss the term "best" and replace it with "good." Because you can't predict what a toddler will do ten or fifteen years hence—or where you might be personally or professionally—when you're saving, you can't possibly know which savings strategy is best.

But, a Coverdell could be a good strategy if:

❑ You meet the income thresholds and are able to contribute.

❑ You have a reasonably strong belief that the intended beneficiary will go to college or will use the money to finance private high school or grammar school.

❑ You earn enough to make sheltering taxable income worthwhile. Naturally, that's a subjective decision that's partly affected by just how averse you are to paying tax. But, economically, it generally does not make sense to shelter income from tax when your capital gains rate will be 10 percent or less. (That's the rate paid by those in the 15 percent marginal tax bracket.) You simply give up too much flexibility for too small a tax reward.

❑ You are fairly certain you will not need to tap this money for any expense outside of education.

❑ You earn enough to make the chance of qualifying for significant student aid unlikely. (See Chapter 11 for guidelines.)

❑ You like having the ability to invest in individual stocks and bonds.

❑ You'd like to trade actively in the college account.

chapter 4

529 Plans

THE LATEST DARLING OF THE COLLEGE SAVINGS WORLD
is the so-called 529 plan. There's good reason for its popularity.
Where most tax-favored college savings plans have income restrictions that bar those who earn more than set amounts from contributing, 529 plans do not. Anyone can contribute—parents, grandparents, aunts, uncles, friends, and others. And the amounts they can contribute are generous. Many plans allow beneficiaries to accumulate up to $250,000 per account before they must stop saving.

In other words, if you want to save big and quickly, Mom, Dad, Aunt Selma, Uncle Fred, Grandma Sherry, and Grandpa George can all kick in to newborn John Jr.'s college fund. Although some of those thoughtful relatives may have only $25 or $50, if Mom and Dad (or the grandparents) are well-heeled, they could *each* contribute up to $55,000 in a single year.

Little Johnny could keep accepting college donations in his 529 plan until the account hit the statewide per-beneficiary limit. That limit varies from state to state but typically hovers between $100,000 and $305,000. If that's not enough to get him through college, money is not the problem.

529 Plans

Maximum contribution —State plan limits, which range from $100,000 (Tennessee) to $305,000 (South Dakota).

Tax benefits —No up-front federal tax deductions, but the money accumulates on a tax-deferred basis.

—Withdrawals used to pay education expenses are federal income tax free.

—Twenty-three states give residents up-front tax deductions on state returns, in addition to tax-free withdrawals. In these states, 529s beat all other savings options for virtually all types of savers by a large margin.

Limitations —To reap the tax rewards, beneficiaries must use the 529 savings for college costs only.

Pros —Can be used by any taxpayer, rich or poor.

—Usually no age limits on beneficiaries, nor income limits on donors.

—If you're not fond of the 529 you've selected, once annually you can roll 529 assets to another state's plan, tax free.

—Particularly valuable for rich taxpayers who want to move a lot of money out of their estates into the college coffers of their children—and even grandchildren and great-, great-grandchildren, or nieces and nephews.

Cons — If the money isn't used for qualified education expenses, it's taxable to the recipient and subject to a 10 percent federal tax penalty when withdrawn. There may be state tax penalties as well.

Tricks — Parents and grandparents who want to contribute a lot in a hurry can put up to $55,000 into a 529 plan for one beneficiary in a single year, without estate- or gift-tax consequences.

Traps — Beware of high account management and maintenance fees.

— All provisions of the 2001 Tax Act are set to expire in 2010, including the tax-free treatment of 529 withdrawals.

The lack of income restrictions on donors and the huge amount that can be saved make 529 plans the best choice for high-income parents who want to prefund their children's education.

But 529 plans can make sense for others, too. Middle- and lower-income parents who want to save for college, but believe their kids may qualify for some student aid—or might not go to college, may find certain aspects of 529 plans highly attractive. Specifically, 529 assets are currently considered the asset of the donor, not the beneficiary. That means that assets held in these plans generally do not reduce the student's eligibility for financial aid as dramatically as assets held in a Coverdell account or an UGMA account (see Chapter 11). In addition, if the child named as the beneficiary of the account decides not to go to college, the donor can redirect the funds to another college-bound recipient.

The investment options offered by these plans can also be attractive for those who like to leave the day-to-day investment choices to somebody else. The plans bear some resemblance to 401(k)s in that participants are generally able to choose among a relative handful of investment options, usually mutual funds. Once you've made an investment selection, you can leave the day-to-day decisions about which stocks or bonds to buy and sell to the manager running the account. Since most plans also allow affordable monthly contributions, they're a great way to put college savings on automatic pilot.

What's a 529?

Like many tax-favored savings plans, such as 401(k)s and 403(b)s, 529 plans are named after the tax-code section that gives them life. However, unlike the retirement savings programs, the federal government's 529 plan was created in response to something that was already happening.

Several states had started college savings and prepaid tuition plans to help parents plan for the rapidly escalating cost of college. These plans gave in-state residents the ability to save for their children's education on a tax-favored basis.

However, the structure of the plans and the tax breaks parents could reap from using state plans varied dramatically. Some plans were a great deal; others were a bust. Moreover, since the rules were all dictated by each individual state, states often placed restrictions on where the plan participant's child could go to college. If the child chose an out-of-state school, the parents were faced with the prospect of simply getting their money back—not always with interest—leaving them right where they started. That added another level of difficulty to the college planning process, since it not only asked parents to predict which type of school their child would aspire to, but which school would *accept* the child some years in the future. Needless to say, parents were perplexed about the viability of the plans.

States wanted the federal government to provide tax incentives to make the plans more attractive. By inviting in the federal government, they also would create national standards. Several federal tax laws were passed over the course of the past decade to give the state plans federal standing.

Then the Economic Growth and Tax Relief Reconciliation Act of 2001 was passed. The act included national standards for state-operated tuition savings programs and federal tax exemptions for money saved in qualifying plans. Since then, the number of plans offered and the amount of money parents have poured into these vehicles has soared. Total assets in 529 plans tripled to $10 billion by the end of 2001, according to a study by Financial Research Corporation. The same study predicts that 529 assets will increase forty-fold by 2010.

Although the tax benefits are just one aspect of 529 savings plans, they're the main reason these plans currently appear to be the belle of the college savings ball. So let's start with how the tax breaks work.

Federal Tax Benefits

Contributions to 529 plans are not deductible on federal returns. But you do not pay income tax on the amount accumulated in the account in any given year, regardless of whether that accumulation was from interest or investment gains. If you opt to sell one investment and buy another—something that would trigger income or capital gains taxes if the money was housed in an ordinary savings account—no tax is due as long as the investments remain under the 529 umbrella.

In addition, if 529 withdrawals are used for qualified education expenses, the money remains tax free on federal returns when withdrawn. Incidentally, all of these tax rules are identical to the rules governing so-called Coverdell accounts, too

What Are "Qualified" Expenses?

Qualified education expenses include tuition, fees, books, supplies, and equipment for attendance at an accredited college or university, including community colleges and some vocational schools. For those attending school at least half time, qualified expenses would also include room and board. The money can also be used for graduate schools and the tuition for continuing education courses.

The law also carves out an exception for "special-needs" children. The exception, while vague, is generally believed to allow tax-free 529 distributions to finance the cost of special-education schools and classes for the developmentally disabled.

These rules are also similar to the rules governing Coverdell accounts. However, where Coverdell accounts also allow withdrawals to finance grammar school and high school costs, 529 plans usually do not without triggering tax and penalties. The only exception to that is for special-needs children, as noted above.

Tax Penalties

What happens if the money is not used for qualified education expenses? The interest or investment earnings become taxable to the recipient of the funds, and he also will owe a 10 percent federal tax penalty on the taxable amount withdrawn. (There may be additional state tax penalties, too.)

For example, let's say someone in the 25 percent federal tax bracket triggered $10,000 in 529 withdrawals and did not use that amount for higher education. Half of the withdrawal was principal and not taxable. The other $5,000 was investment returns. He'd pay 35 percent in federal income tax on the taxable portion of this distribution, which works out to $1,750. He may also face state tax and state tax penalties.

Contribution Limits

Where 529 plans begin to differentiate themselves from Coverdell accounts is with the contribution limits. There is no federal restriction on how much can be contributed to these plans.

Federal law says only that the contribution limits set by the states must somehow relate to the total cost of college education. Some states have interpreted that to include the all-in costs of tuition, books, fees, room, board, transportation, and miscellaneous expenses for four years of school. Some have added in the cost of graduate programs. The bottom line: Every state allows 529 plans to accept at least $100,000 per beneficiary. Some allow contributions exceeding $300,000 per beneficiary. (For a full state-by-state list of contribution limits and contact information for the various state plans, see Chapter 15.)

Another distinction between 529s and Coverdells: There are no income restrictions on contributors. On the other hand, anyone earning more than $110,000 when single, or $220,000 when married, cannot contribute to a Coverdell account. If you want to contribute to a 529 plan, it doesn't matter how wealthy you are. Rich folks can deposit with reckless abandon.

State Tax Benefits

The state tax benefits of contributing to a 529 account in states that impose an income tax vary from pretty good to remarkable. Virtually every state exempts withdrawals from state income tax, if the money is used for qualified education expenses as defined by the federal government. Money that accumulates in the account is also tax deferred, just as it is on federal returns. That can provide a solid tax benefit.

Where the tax breaks get remarkable is in the twenty-three states that actually provide up-front tax deductions for all or a portion of contributions to a 529 plan. For instance, Colorado offers an unlimited deduction for 529 contributions on state tax returns. Since withdrawals won't be taxed either, that gives something of a double-dip benefit. Other states allow a limited deduction. Georgia, for example, allows a $2,000 deduction on state tax returns for 529 contributions. Louisiana allows a $2,400 state tax deduction per year, per beneficiary. Michigan allows a $5,000 annual deduction for single filers and a deduction up to $10,000 for a married couple.

Which states offer up-front deductions for 529 contributions? Colorado, Georgia, Idaho, Illinois, Iowa, Kansas, Louisiana, Maryland, Michigan, Mississippi, Missouri, Montana, Nebraska, New Mexico, New York, Ohio, Oklahoma, Oregon, South Carolina, Utah, Virginia, West Virginia, and Wisconsin.

Up-front state tax deductions aside, the biggest tax benefit you get from a 529 is the ability to let your earnings grow on a tax-free basis. Given enough time—and decent investment returns—that benefit is worth thousands of dollars.

But, the less time and money you have invested, the less valuable the tax break. Let's consider a few hypothetical examples to illustrate how the tax breaks work out in dollars and cents.

Wealthy parents. Susan and James Vestibule, who earn $250,000 annually, are saving for their twin sons, Tyler and Timon, age 2. They plunk $20,000 for each toddler—$40,000 total—into their state's 529 plan, which is able to return 8 percent on average annually.

On their eighteenth birthdays, each little Vestibule has $68,519 in his account. The Vestibules plan to use that money to pay for their first semester at Princeton. (Just kidding; $68,000 should be enough to pay for *at least* two semesters even sixteen years from now ... we hope.) Since all the money will be used for education, the $48,519 in investment earnings will never be taxed. Naturally, neither will the principal.

Given today's capital gains rate of 20 percent, that should save the Vestibules more than $9,700 in federal income tax for each child, or roughly $19,400 total, compared to saving the money in the parents' names in a taxable account. Moreover, they save on state income taxes, too.

If the Vestibules' state normally imposed a 6 percent tax, the tax-free nature of 529 withdrawals would cut the Vestibules' state tax bill by $5,822 at the time of withdrawal. If they live in one of the twenty-three states that allow a tax deduction for all or a portion of 529 contributions, the tax savings are even better.

By reducing their income by $40,000 in the year that they contributed to Tyler and Timon's accounts, the Vestibules cut $2,400 off their state tax bill. Combine the up-front and back-end tax savings and their total tax savings amount to a whopping $27,622—nearly two-thirds of their original contribution of $40,000 to the kids' accounts.

But, even if the Vestibules' state doesn't offer an up-front deduction, their total federal and state tax savings in this example amount to $25,222—more than half of the Vestibules' initial investment. To put it another way, the net, after-tax, cost of this investment was $14,777 ($7,388 per toddler), and it generated $137,038 in college money. That's not half bad.

Middle-income families. The economics are not as compelling for middle-income families with older children, though. That's simply because their money doesn't have enough time to earn tax-free investment returns.

Consider Jane and Joe Johnson, who earn $80,000 together and don't have the discretionary income to drop big dollars into any type of savings. They decide to set aside $100 a month for each of their two children, Mary and Megan, who are 8 and 10. They, too, are able to earn 8 percent annually on their 529 savings.

When Megan is 18, she has $13,387 saved, $9,600 of which is the principal that her parents put into the account. The Johnsons avoided $757 in capital gains taxes on the $3,787 profit in Megan's account by putting it into a 529 plan rather than an ordinary investment account. Assuming they also avoid 6 percent in state income taxes, they reap another $227 in tax savings, for a total of $984.

The profit in Mary's account is slightly bigger—about $6,295. (Because they saved two extra years with Mary, her account is worth $18,295 when she hits college age, but $12,000 of the amount is the Johnsons' principal.) With Mary, the Johnsons save $1,295 in capital gains taxes and $378 in state taxes for a $1,673 total.

The Bad News

Unfortunately, those who fund *all* of their college expenses with savings from a 529 plan cannot claim education-oriented tax credits, such as the Hope tax credit and the lifetime learning credit.

That's no loss to the Vestibules because they're too rich to claim these credits anyway. The credits are income tested, so those who earn more than $41,000 if single or $82,000 if married, filing jointly, need not apply. (This 2002 threshold has been adjusted for inflation, increasing by roughly $1,000 per year.)

But it's an issue for the Johnsons. Tax credits offset federal income tax bills on a dollar-for-dollar basis, so they can be highly lucrative. If the Johnsons funded *all* of their girls' college bills with the 529 accounts, they would have to forgo roughly $4,339 in tax credits over the course of Megan's education, and roughly $4,830 in tax credits over the course of Mary's schooling. Since the 529 plans saved the Johnsons a total of $2,657 in taxes ($984 for Megan and $1,673 for Mary), that would put them $6,512 behind.

But there's a trick to this that might make 529 savings worthwhile, if the Johnson girls' total school expenses—including room, board, transportation, books, and supplies—amounted to more than what they'd saved in the 529 plan.

This gets a little complicated, so bear with me. The Hope tax credit and the lifetime learning credits can be claimed only for tuition and fee expenses. Meanwhile, tax-free distributions from 529 plans can be used for tuition, fees, books, transportation, and room and board for students attending school at least half time.

If the 529 savings are dedicated to paying room and board, while the parents tap other assets to pay tuition and fees, they can claim *both* the tax exemption for the 529 income *and* the tax credit. If your income is below the tax credit thresholds above, be sure to read Chapter 10, on pay-as-you-go tax breaks, carefully.

Transferability and Control

What happens if you've saved $20,000 in a 529 account for your daughter Jane, but Jane grows up and doesn't want to go to college? Instead, she decides to become a beautician. Beauty college is located just down the street. So, Jane lives at home and pays just $2,000 in tuition for her entire beauty training. You've got $18,000 in savings left. And, thanks to Jane, your hair looks *fabulous.*

Now you have to make a decision. The 529 rules allow you to transfer the assets that you saved for Jane to another beneficiary. There are some restrictions on tax-free transfers, however. The new beneficiary must be a family member of the original beneficiary. Naturally, the government doesn't trust you to define "family," so they have a handy definition for you to use.

The new beneficiary must be: A spouse, son, daughter, or descendant of any of the above. It could be a stepdaughter or stepson; a stepbrother or stepsister; father, mother, stepfather or stepmother or any ancestor of the beneficiary's parents. It could be a child of a brother or sister; a brother or sister of the father or mother; a son-in-law, daughter-in-law, mother-in-law, father-in-law, brother-in-law, or the spouse of any of the foregoing. Ahem.

If you have another child who needs the money for college, you may decide to transfer the money to him. Or, if you're particularly close to any of these other relatives, you could enrich their college coffers with Jane's leftover savings. In any event, the donor retains control over the distribution of the 529 assets.

Exercising Control

Does this mean that you can dictate which school your child attends by controlling the purse strings? In other words, if your child decided to pursue a course of study that was not to your liking, could you deny him access to the 529 savings that you accumulated for him? The law does not specifically say, but it currently appears that you could.

As with all powers, this can be used for good—to deter a child from attending Drug Culture University, which would have sent him into a life-long tailspin. Or for bad—to punish a child who refuses to attend the university of your choice and become a doctor, because that's what you've always wanted.

Either way, realize that if you opt to exert this type of control, you're nearly certain to trigger resentment and anger. If you need to do this to protect your child, do it. But if you're doing it to control your child, realize that you, the donor, are an overbearing jerk. Seek counseling.

What about Jane?

Assuming that you're not angry with Jane for putting green high-lights in Grandma's hair, you may want to consider the fairness issue before you start doing what tax rules allow by transferring that money to another college-bound recipient.

You saved that money for Jane, right? Was it to be used only for college, or are you willing to say that you wanted that money to give Jane more options in her life? If so, you can let Jane hang onto the account for the day when she has children of her own who may want to go to college, or beauty school. If Jane does not touch the money and leaves it for her children's schooling, there will be no tax penalties.

The other option: You can let Jane keep the money and, perhaps, use it to set herself up in business or maybe buy a house. If you choose this option, she will be subject to income taxes and tax penalties on the taxable distribution from this account.

On the federal income tax side, that means that the part of the account that's interest and investment earnings is taxable at her ordinary income tax rate, plus 10 percent.

Estate Tax Considerations

Whenever you are giving money to anyone—be it a child, grandchild, niece, nephew, or friend—you must be aware of the possible estate- or gift-tax implications. If you give less than $11,000 annually to any individual, you have no worries. You can give an unlimited number of people gifts of up to $11,000 annually, and no estate or gift tax will be imposed on you or them.

But if you give more than $11,000 annually to any one recipient, there is normally a tax that must be assessed either now or later. There is an exception for 529 plans, however. As noted above, you can give one recipient up to five years worth of $11,000 annual gifts in just one year—$55,000 total—without triggering estate or gift taxes. However, you may not give that same recipient more money over the next five years, unless you want to run afoul of Uncle Sam. (Sure, you can still buy that same child Christmas gifts and take her to the movies, but if your continued generosity is more than the "de minimus" sort, contact a tax adviser to determine the implications.)

However, if you die within that five-year period, a portion of the gift will be added back into your estate to determine whether or not your estate will have to pay taxes on the amount. In other words, if you die two years after putting $55,000 in your grandchild's 529 account, $33,000 of that amount will be counted as part of your estate for federal estate tax purposes.

If you are very wealthy and a seemingly long way from death, you can use 529 plans to set up an education legacy for your family. For instance, you could set up 529 plans for each of your grandchildren, fund them to the maximum amount the law allows, and hope that any money that grandchild doesn't use for education, she could use to fund the education of her children and her children's children.

Anyone contemplating such a generous act should seek the services of a competent estate planning attorney, however. There are other ways to fund education for your heirs, at least while you're alive. You may want to explore all the possible options—and the potential repercussions for the other aspects of your estate plan—before you settle on a course.

A Caveat

It is important to emphasize that all of the provisions in the 2001 Tax Act currently are set to expire in 2010. That includes the tax-free treatment of 529 withdrawals. Many tax experts believe this provision will be "extended" and that 529 withdrawals will remain tax-free forever. However, little about the U.S. tax law is truly predictable. If the current 529 tax exemption does expire in 2010, the law says that withdrawals made after that date will be taxed at the child's rate.

Account Set-Up

How do you set up a 529? Generally, it's just like setting up a mutual fund or bank account. You'll need to fill out a few forms with the institution of your choice. Those forms are likely to ask for information about you and the beneficiary of the account. In many cases, it will also ask how you would like the 529 assets to be invested. (In some cases, that decision will be made for you by the plan, which will use a formula based on your assets and the number of years left before the beneficiary hits college age.)

Then you can decide whether to fund the account with a single gift or with monthly or annual contributions. Virtually all 529 plans operating today accept both. (For information about minimum and maximum contribution limits to each state's plan, see the resource directory in Chapter 15.)

One 529 per Beneficiary

What if you have lots of children or grandchildren and you want to save for them all? Unfortunately, you can't set up a "master" 529 that could fund everyone's education. Generally, you have to set up one 529 per beneficiary. You can change the beneficiary later, if the named beneficiary doesn't go to college or doesn't need all of the money, but the plans are set up to accommodate just one beneficiary at a time.

Picking among the Plethora of 529s

The big challenge is deciding where to open your 529. The reason: You can open an account with any state's plan. It doesn't matter where you or the beneficiary lives, nor where the beneficiary attends school. That gives you a dizzying array of options. Not only do all fifty states offer a 529 plan—or have one in the works—many states offer several choices and more are being launched each week. You may decide to stick with your own state's plan, or you may find that another state offers better investment choices, higher contribution limits, or lower fees—any of which might tip the balance.

How do you choose the best plan for you and your intended beneficiary? Here are six key factors to consider:

1   **State tax deductions:** If you live in one of the twenty-three states that provide up-front tax deductions, that deduction can provide a compelling reason to stick with your own state's plan. Generally speaking, you cannot take an up-front tax deduction for contributing to a plan that's not in your state of residence. Naturally, the precise benefit of contributing to your own state's tax-deductible plan will be determined by your state's tax rate, how much you earn, how much you contribute, and whether the state offers a full or partial deduction for that contribution. But if you figure that you pay 5 percent in state taxes, a $10,000 contribution that's fully deductible saves you $500 on your state income tax bill.

2   **Fees:** There are five types of fees that *can* be charged on 529 accounts: A set-up or enrollment fee, an annual account maintenance fee, a "load" or sales charge that pays the broker who sells the plan, annual investment-management fees, and annual mutual-fund expenses. However, most of these fees are discretionary.

Only one fee is always charged. That's the annual investment management fee charged by the mutual fund that's handling the money. It pays a fund manager to buy and sell shares and keep track of whether the fund's investment choices are balanced in the way that the fund has promised. This fee can range from a low of about 0.30 percent of the account value to more than 2 percent of the account value.

All other things being equal, the lower the fees, the better. Let's take these fees one at a time:

Enrollment fees: These are sometimes charged by the state to cover the cost of the paperwork required to set up the account. They're one-time and generally minor charges—about $30.

Account maintenance fees: These fees are also usually minor—$10 to $30 annually—and usually are waived if the donor funds the account through regular automatic contributions, or if the amount invested exceeds certain thresholds.

Loads: A load is a sales charge that can be paid either in a single, up-front lump sum or through regular fees charged on the value of the account—or a combination of both. The load is paid to the broker who sells you this investment. It doesn't do anything for you, but it ensures that your broker can eat, keep a roof over his head, finance private schools for his children, and make payments on his BMW.

If you need a broker because you desperately need advice, consider this money well spent. But, keep an eye on your pocketbook. These fees add up and can have a dramatic impact on the value of your savings.

Consider this: If you are investing $10,000 in a college savings plan that has a 3.5 percent load and a 0.75 percent annual sales charge, your initial investment is immediately cut to $9,650, which is the value after the up-front load is subtracted. But that immediate $350 hit pales in comparison to what you'll pay over time because of the insidious 0.75 percent annual sales charge.

Figuring the impact of that 0.75 percent annual fee is a little more complicated. The best way to do it is to look at the total value of the account over time with—and without—that charge. Figuring that the underlying investments return 10 percent and you invest for ten years, your investment will be worth $23,374 when you figure in the 0.75 percent sales fee. If you didn't pay the sales fees, and earned the same return on the account, your account value would be $25,937.42 instead. Total cost of this load: $2,562.95.

Again, this is just the cost of advice. You haven't yet paid the investment management fees.

Annual management and mutual-fund fees: Some plans charge a fee to monitor the investment choices. Others charge a separate fee to manage the investments inside the mutual fund. Still others blend these fees together. These fees are expressed as a percentage of the account value, which means the higher the fee, the less investment return you'll enjoy in the end.

All things being equal, choose the plan that charges the lowest fees.

Don't some investment managers do a better job of investing your money, and thus earn their higher fees? Some investment managers do a better job than others, but there has never been any evidence suggesting that those who charge higher fees do a better job. In fact, most studies indicate the opposite. Fees are the best determinant of how a fund will perform for its owners. The lower the fees, the better the final return to account owners.

Fees are, in fact, such a huge issue that the Securities and Exchange Commission has an investment evaluator on its website that will help you compare mutual fund investments based on the fees they charge. This Web-based calculator at www.sec.gov, was designed for mutual funds, not 529 plans. But, it will work just fine to compare 529 plans, too. If somebody's trying to talk you into a high-cost fund, definitely check it out. It's under the heading titled "Investor Information." Click on Interactive Tools and then on Mutual Fund Cost Calculator.

3 **Investment options:** 529 plans offer a limited number of investment choices, just like the 401(k) plan that you've probably got at work. In some cases, in fact, there's just one investment choice. It's likely to be a blend of both stock and bonds, mixed in quantities that the plan considers appropriate, based on the age of the child who is named the beneficiary of the account.

Other plans offer several investment choices. With these plans, you generally are allowed to choose between fixed income (bonds and savings accounts); equities (company stocks); blended accounts, which mix both stocks and bonds; or the pre-mixed age-based solution. (More details on the pros and cons of various 529 investment options appear in Chapter 6.)

What 529s currently don't allow is the ability to buy individual stocks or bonds through the accounts. Generally speaking, if you buy a 529, you are leaving the day-to-day investment choices to a fund manager. Your investment control is limited to what's available through the plan. If you hate the plan's choices, you can transfer your 529 assets to another state's plan without tax penalty once a year. (You're allowed to make more than one yearly transfer if you change the named beneficiary of the account.)

If you want more investment control than a 529 plan allows, consider opening a Coverdell education savings account instead. These offer virtually limitless investment choices.

4 **Contribution choices:** You can always open a 529 plan with a single large deposit. However, some plans also allow you to open an account with as little as $25 or $50, as long as you promise to contribute more through automatic monthly deposits. Some plans also accept small additional contributions that you make at irregular intervals.

If you don't have a big chunk of cash, you'll want to find a plan that allows the monthly option. If you have other relatives who might want to pitch in money at birthdays or holidays, look for a 529 that accepts contributions at any point and in any denomination.

5 **Flexibility:** Because 529 plans are essentially an outgrowth of state savings plans, which were set up before national 529 legislation was enacted, a few plans have funky restrictions. Some, for instance, won't allow you to leave money saved for a beneficiary who has reached a certain age. If you think you'll have the assets and the inclination to leave 529 money saved for long periods—perhaps to provide a long-term education legacy for your heirs—ask about whether there is any limit on the age of the beneficiary or the amount of time that the money can be left in the plan.

6 **Bells and whistles:** While it's not the most important consideration, finding a plan that suits the way you like to invest will make you more satisfied in the end. Once you've narrowed your 529 choices down to a relative handful that all look equally acceptable, check for the service features that matter to you. For instance, if you're a computer enthusiast and track all your investments electronically, make sure the 529 you choose offers Web-based account management. If you do all

your investing by phone, make sure the 529 offers a toll-free phone line and reasonable service hours. Also call the line a few times to see if there's a long wait to talk to a person who can answer your questions. If you are particularly fond of a particular investment company, ask them if they offer a 529. The choices are vast. You can find one to suit you perfectly.

State-by-State Details

Are you convinced that a 529 is the right choice, but want to know details of every state's plan so you can choose the best option? Point your Web browser to www.savingforcollege.com. This website is operated by a man named Joseph Hurley, who has written extensively on 529 plans. The site goes through each option in each state with vivid detail, chronicling which states offer tax deductions, which fund companies manage which plans, what they charge, the investment options they provide, and how to reach them.

Better yet, Hurley gives each plan "cap" ratings—one rating for in-state residents and another for out-of-state residents considering the plan. Five caps means excellent; one cap is poor. If the plan has no caps, don't even go there.

There's also a 529 website operated by the College Savings Plan Network, an association of state treasurers who hope to clarify the rules governing state college savings plans. The site, www .collegesavings.org, offers links to each state's plan and their toll-free phone numbers. But it's not as easy to navigate as Hurley's site, nor does it give recommendations similar to Hurley's cap ratings.

Those who don't have Web access should consider buying Hurley's book, *The Best Way to Save for College: A Complete Guide to 529 Plans* (BonaCom Publications, 2002, current list price: $26.95). It's sure to save you a fortune in both time and trouble. Hurley is simply the most authoritative, unbiased source in the industry. A certified public accountant and author of three books on the topic, Hurley has opened 529 accounts in twenty-three states for his two children. By opening so many accounts, Hurley is able to evaluate both what the plans say and what they do. That makes it possible for him to provide a wealth of information for you.

(Just in case you're curious, this author and publishing house have no economic or personal interest in Joseph Hurley's business. This recommendation is unsolicited and sincere.)

Prepaid Tuition Plans

More than a dozen states offer so-called prepaid tuition plans. They are not 529s, but they are similar enough that it makes sense to address them here.

These plans are similar to 529s in that you set them up through your state Treasurer's office, and they are aimed at funding college education. In many states, these plans were the precursors to 529 plans. But that's where the similarities stop.

Comparing prepaid tuition plans to 529 plans is almost like comparing a 401(k) to a defined benefit pension. With a 401(k) you know how much you've got saved at any given moment in time. With a defined benefit pension, you usually don't—and you don't care. You simply have a promise of a future benefit. Today's value of that benefit is almost incidental.

What They Are

Generally, prepaid tuition plans provide an up-front guarantee. If you invest a set amount of money in the plan by a set age, your child will have his state college tuition 100 percent paid. Period. Guaranteed. It doesn't matter how much state tuition bills rise in the interim. It doesn't matter which state university your child chooses. It's a done deal. The bill is paid. You can relax.

Those who can't afford to plop down a full payment for four years of school can pay over time; or, in many cases, they're given the option of buying something less—say, a year's worth of tuition and fees, or even a set number of college unit credits. Again, no matter what those units cost down the line, most states guarantee that you'll never have to pay extra regardless of how much tuition prices rise in the meantime.

What They're Not

Good deal? Maybe. The problem with prepaid tuition plans has always been just one thing: your child. Generally, these plans are affordable for those who contribute when the child is a toddler. But, naturally, that's far too soon to know whether the child is college-bound or state school material.

State prepaid tuition plans generally do not pay private college expenses. They also do not guarantee that your child will get into the state school of his or her choice.

What happens if you buy a prepaid tuition contract and your child can't get into one of the state schools that are covered by the contract? It depends. In some cases, the plan will pay an amount equivalent to the state school costs to whatever college or university your child does attend. In other cases, the plan will refund your deposit, plus interest. In others, they may simply refund all, or a portion, of what you put in.

In other words, these are not flexible investment savings plans like 529s. They can be very effective in doing what they say they'll do—paying the cost of in-state tuition at a public college or university. But, how well they'll work in your life will vary dramatically based on your individual circumstances. Unfortunately, some of those circumstances are hard to predict.

Evaluating a Prepaid Plan

Because there is so much variation in what is offered by the states that still sponsor prepaid tuition plans, it's incumbent on the parent to investigate the details.

What should you know? According to Hurley, who lists prepaid tuition plans on his website, these are some of the questions parents should ask:

❏ Is your child likely to go to one of the schools sponsored by the plan? Although it's a tricky question, if you seriously consider a prepaid tuition plan, you must at least attempt to guess which college or university your child is likely to attend. Is that school's bills paid by the tuition plan?

❏ What is the cost of the plan versus the current cost of tuition at the target school? To get the current cost of tuition, go to the College Board website at www.collegeboard.com.

❏ What will happen to your money if your child chooses a college that's not on the plan? Will you get your money back? Will you get interest on the money? Will there be a cancellation fee or penalty?

❏ What happens if you change your mind about the plan, before the child even reaches college age? Can you cancel the contract and get your money back? At least one state, Michigan, won't refund the fees until after the child reaches the age of 18, Hurley said.

❏ What happens if the plan itself becomes insolvent? Some are backed by the full faith and credit of the state treasury. Others are not.

❏ What happens if the plan earns a fortune on its money—far more than anticipated based on the fees you were charged and far more than is necessary to pay the public school expenses covered by the plan? Will the plan share the excess with existing participants, or does the windfall simply support the program or state?

❏ Will the plan allow you to roll over your prepaid tuition balance into a 529 plan? If so, how would the balance of your account be determined?

More Info

If prepaid plans sound like something you'd like to consider, point your Web browser to www.savingforcollege.com and look up your state. Generally speaking, you may only participate in a prepaid plan if you are a resident of the state that offers it, or if the beneficiary is a resident of that state. Unlike 529 plans, you generally may not buy a prepaid contract from another state's plan.

chapter 5

Call Me Ugh-Ma*

*apologies to Herman Melville

THEY USED TO BE THE ONLY GAME IN TOWN. NOW THEY'RE considered last year's technology. And a lot of parents feel like they're stuck with their old UGMA accounts because they were disciplined enough to save before Congress decided to get so generous with all sorts of new tax-favored savings plans for college.

There are some benefits to investing in UGMA accounts that are overlooked in these days of new and improved options. It is true that today UGMAs are no longer the best way to save for school. Still, it's a good idea to know how they work, so you can make an educated decision. Just what is an UGMA and how does it compare to the new college savings plans?

Uniform Gift to Minors Act (UGMA) accounts, also known as Uniform Transfers to Minors Act (UTMA) accounts, are not specifically meant to be college savings plans. They were designed simply as a vehicle to allow parents and others to give financial gifts, often stocks, to young children. In effect, the UGMA is a simple trust, in which the adult manages assets owned by the child until the child is old enough to take legal control of his own money.

Uniform Gift to Minors Act (UGMA)

Maximum contribution —No maximum, but you are taxed on contributions of more than $11,000 per year to any one beneficiary.

Tax benefits —Income earned within the account is taxable to the child at the child's presumably rock-bottom income tax rate.

Limitations —If a child under the age of 14 earns more than $1,500 in realized investment gains in any one year, his earnings are taxed at his parent's higher rates.

—An income tax form must be filed for any year in which stocks or bonds have been sold in the child's account triggering more than $750 in gains.

—When money is withdrawn, any previously untaxed earnings become taxable at the child's rate.

Pros —UGMA assets can be used for any purpose that's in the child's interest.

Cons —Any money placed in an UGMA account is considered a completed gift. It is the property of the child. At the age of majority—usually either age 18 or 21, depending on state law—the child can claim control over it.

Tricks —Over time you can contribute enough to your minor's account to "emancipate" her, allowing her to pay the cost of her own living expenses. This can provide children of wealthy parents the ability to claim income-tested tax breaks that their parents wouldn't be able to touch.

Traps — Usually not the best choice for anyone but the well-heeled.

—Middle- and lower-income parents whose children may qualify for financial aid could see that aid reduced because of savings in an UGMA account. The aid cost is potentially higher than the tax breaks that middle- and lower-income families are likely to reap by having money in the kids' names.

Opening an UGMA

When an adult opens an UGMA account on behalf of a minor, he will fill out a form that asks for information about both the adult "custodian" and the minor. In some instances, it will ask at what age the custodianship will terminate—in other words, the age at which the adult transfers control of the assets to the child.

In addition, new account documents require Social Security numbers for the adult and the child, and note that the account is being opened under the UGMA or UTMA laws in the relevant state.

These accounts can be opened at banks, brokerage firms, mutual-fund companies, credit unions, and other types of financial institutions. Minimum balance requirements at brokerage and mutual-fund companies are often lower for UGMA and UTMA accounts than for standard accounts opened by adults, which allows parents, grandparents, aunts, uncles, or other interested friends to start saving, even if they can't afford a lot.

UGMA Mantra

The moment you transfer money into an UGMA or UTMA account, you need to chant this mantra: "The money belongs to the child ... The money belongs to the child ... The money belongs to the child ..."

Money transferred into an UGMA or UTMA is a *completed gift*, just like baby clothes or games or anything else that you give to a child with no hope of ever getting it back. I mention this only because when it comes to financial assets, that appears to be a tough concept for many an adult to swallow. After all, you still have investment control over the assets, don't you? Doesn't that mean you can take the money back, if the child doesn't live up to what you see as her end of the bargain? No.

The gift is truly a gift. You can't hold it up as a carrot, requiring certain behavior before it can be claimed. The only thing the child must do to claim her money is to reach a certain age. That age is usually set by state law—typically either age 18 or age 21—but sometimes it is determined by custodial documents. In any event, it's not determined by whether your daughter attends college, marries a person to your liking, gets good grades, stays out of prison, or kicks drugs. If you want to give money with strings attached, you need a real trust and a lawyer, not an UGMA account.

Once the money is in an UGMA or UTMA account, it belongs to the child. You are only a steward, ensuring that the money stays safe and is properly invested until the child reaches the applicable age at which she is deemed old enough to manage the investment accounts herself. The money is no longer yours. It belongs to the child . . . it belongs to the child . . . it belongs to the child.

Taxation of UGMA Assets

An UGMA is not a tax-favored account. Interest earned within these accounts, as well as capital gains recognized when securities are sold, are fully taxable at the time they are realized. They are, however, taxable at the child's rate, which is often low.

Young children pay no tax on investment earnings of less than $750 per year. That's the standard deduction that can be claimed by someone who is also claimed as a dependent on another taxpayer's return in 2002. The next $750 in annual investment earnings is taxed at the child's rate, probably 10 percent, unless the child is an actor or entrepreneur earning other income. However, any investment income exceeding $1,500 annually earned by a child *under the age of 14* is taxed at the parent's marginal tax rate.

This provision is designed to stop very wealthy parents from transferring vast stockpiles of assets into the names of their children to get the benefit of the child's lower income tax rate. However, the practical effect is this: If your son realizes earnings of about 5 percent on his investments, he shouldn't have more than about $30,000 in his name until after he's 14. After that, so-called kiddie tax rules no longer apply. At that point, no matter how much he earns, he's taxed at his own rate.

Realize, however, that the $1,500 limitation is on realized earnings. If he has all his money in an index fund, which throws off taxable earnings equivalent to about 1.5 percent of asset value each year, he doesn't have to worry about kiddie taxes unless his savings account exceeds $100,000, or unless his custodian starts actively trading shares and realizing taxable profits.

What Is It Good For?

UGMA accounts remain a great way to transfer assets to a child when you have no idea what he is going to want to do with the money. If you *know* that the child is headed to college, an UGMA is not the best choice for his college savings. On the other hand, if you think he may want to start a business, or want some time to "find himself" between high school and college, or need to emancipate himself from his home situation, an UGMA is not a bad idea. It gives the child and the donor huge flexibility, both in how the assets are invested and in how they're used.

UGMA and UTMA accounts are governed by state law, so there are some minor variations, but generally the only restriction on money coming out of these accounts is that it must be used for the minor's benefit. Naturally, getting a college education is to the minor's benefit, but so is getting a car or getting out and about, in the right circumstances.

... As a Teaching Tool

If you aim to teach a child about investing, an UGMA is also a good option because it is both flexible and has consequences. No other type of child's account can show a kid the impact of buying and selling a growth stock, for instance.

To understand why, you have to consider the limitations of the other savings options. There are significant limits on your investment choices in a 529 plan, which make them a poor choice for those aiming to school their children on the risks and rewards of buying and selling individual securities. Coverdell accounts provide more investing choices. You can, for example, buy and sell individual stocks within these accounts. But, as is also true with 529 plans, there would be no tax consequences for buying and selling investments inside the Coverdell account. Since taxes typically take away at least 10 percent to 20 percent of your investment return, any investment lesson that ignores taxes ignores a lot.

The tax lesson isn't confined to those wishing to buy stocks, either. There are vast differences in the tax consequences of buying an actively managed mutual fund versus an index fund. Index funds are called "passively" managed because the fund managers do very little trading, which means the fund passes on fewer taxable capital gains during any given year. Meanwhile, bonds generate income that's taxable at ordinary income tax rates. For those who want to teach as well as transfer, an UGMA is a good choice, at least for a portion of the child's assets.

UGMA for Schooling

There are some detriments to using UGMA savings to finance college. The biggest such detriment is that student-aid formulas count assets held in a child's name with much greater weight than assets held in a parent's name. In short, aid formulas figure that roughly one-third of UGMA or UTMA assets will be used to finance the child's schooling each year. If the money had been in the parents' names, only about 5 percent of it would be considered an asset that could be tapped for college education.

On the bright side, if you have UGMA assets set aside for your daughter, Suzy, they *do not count* as your asset or an asset belonging to your son, Tommy, when Tommy applies to college. So, a family that has significant savings for both of their two children—or even relatively modest college funds for each of their ten children—would see some benefit to having these assets in UGMA accounts, rather than in a 529 plan or another account in the parent's names.

Consider, for example, the hypothetical O'Brien family: parents Maureen and Ryan, and their ten tykes—Timmy Patrick, Molly, Michael, Brian, Colleen, Daniel, Matthew, William, and Raymond. Maureen and Ryan have put $5,000 aside for each child's college bills, a total of $50,000. However, the money is in individual UGMA accounts in each child's name.

When it comes time to figuring out student aid, each child effectively pays full freight on his own savings—aid formulas expect them to spend about one-third of their own savings, that's about $1,750 in the first year on college bills. But the other $45,000 held in the names of this student's siblings is not assessed at all. If the savings for all the children were in the parents' names, it could reduce the family's need assessment by as much as $2,800 per year.

Aid formulas do account for multiple students, so if all ten—or even the first five—O'Briens were in college at the same time, the family's need assessment would rise. But if Timmy and Patrick decided to start their own business with the $10,000 that their parents set aside for them, Molly would not be penalized for their savings when she enrolled at Notre Dame.

Have UGMA; Don't Want It

But you don't have ten kids, and the benefits of teaching your child to invest don't impress you? All of your kids are college-bound, so you're not interested in having the UGMA to set Timmy and Patrick up in industry? In fact, you started an UGMA simply as a way to finance school, and you're now horrified at the impact it might have on the child's ability to qualify for financial aid? At this point, you have two options: Spend or transfer.

Spending the UGMA

If your child is at least two years from college, and you have legitimate expenses that would benefit the child, you have the option of draining the UGMA account—rather than your ordinary savings account—to buy these items.

For instance, let's say that your son, Peter, is 16 and needs a car to get to school and work. You were planning to help him buy a car by kicking in $1,000 or $2,000 for the down payment. Instead of taking that money out of your account, take it out of Peter's UGMA. This is a perfectly legitimate expense for his benefit. Meanwhile, it reduces his dedicated savings for financial aid purposes. Plus, you have $1,000 to $2,000 more in your own name that you can tap to pay for college down the road.

Could you drain the UGMA to pay the rent? The family water bill? Buy groceries? In most states, there's no clear guidance, but probably not. The UGMA account isn't supposed to pay your bills or the bills of your other children. Only in unusual circumstances—a parent lost his job and couldn't keep a roof over the family's collective heads—could you argue that tapping the UGMA assets to pay the rent or mortgage was a legitimate expense that was in the child's best interest.

Notably, it is extremely unusual for UGMA expenditures to be questioned by tax authorities or the children who own the accounts, but it's possible. Make sure you keep records of what you did and can justify the expenses on moral or legal grounds.

Clearly acceptable uses of UGMA assets would be to buy the child a car, a personal computer, or to pay private grammar or high school expenses. Pay for the prom dress or limo? Maybe. But, as with any other spending, don't go hog-wild, especially if your goal is to restructure how you're saving for college rather than to eliminate the college account altogether.

Simply put, you shouldn't spend more of the UGMA assets than you plan to set aside elsewhere in your own name. If the expenditure is something you wouldn't normally tap your own savings for, think twice. You don't want to undo the good thing you started by saving for your child's schooling just because it might cost you some financial aid dollars. Yes, $1 saved in your child's name will cost him about thirty-five cents in aid eligibility during his first year of college. But if you spent that $1 and didn't replace it with other savings for him to use, your UGMA spending strategy set the child back by at least sixty-five cents for every dollar you frittered away.

Transfer to a 529

There's good news and bad news. You can transfer UGMA assets into a 529 plan. But the law does not allow you to recharacterize the ownership of those assets. In other words, assets that were in the UGMA remain in the child's name when they're transferred into a 529 plan.

That means they will still count against the child when it comes time to figure student aid. On the bright side, the taxable income generated in the account while it grows will not be immediately taxable. In fact, it won't be taxable at all, if the child eventually uses the savings for college.

But if you have owned the UGMA for some time and have unrealized capital gains built up in the account, there's more bad news. *You must sell the UGMA assets before buying into the 529.* Why? 529 plans accept only cash investments. (Yes, cash includes checks. It just doesn't include Microsoft stock.)

The bottom line: If you transfer assets from an UGMA to a 529, you are likely to take a tax hit in the process. There are times when this still may make sense. When the profit in the UGMA account is small, the tax hit will be nonexistent or minimal, for instance. It also may make sense to transfer assets into a 529 if the child is very young. That would allow him to avoid future tax obligations on the existing savings.

It *does not* make sense to transfer UGMA assets into a 529 for a sixteen-year-old. The only tax benefit that child would receive from the 529 is the future tax-free treatment of investment earnings. Unless this child's custodian has an investment secret that the rest of us have missed, it's highly unlikely that this account will earn enough in investment returns over that two-year period to make paying tax on the sale of the UGMA assets worthwhile. Moreover, the 529 structure puts restrictions on the use of funds in the account. It makes sense to accept these restrictions only when you'll be getting something of significant value in return.

However, if your UGMA was for an infant—or if you had as many losses as gains, so that you're not concerned about the tax impact—and you decide to transfer, you'll open a so-called UGMA 529. That name tells aid authorities that the 529 is the property of the child, not the donor. Otherwise, the account is treated the same as any other 529. Still, because an UGMA 529 will cost the child more in future aid dollars than a regular 529, you should *not add to this particular 529 from non-UGMA assets.* If you want to put more money in the child's college coffers, open a separate 529 account so that you can preserve the beneficial student-aid treatment for your additional savings.

UGMAs and Estate Planning

There's one other caveat for grandparents who aim to transfer assets to grandchildren through UGMA accounts. If you name yourself as the custodian, a glitch in the estate planning law is likely to place these assets back in your estate if you happen to die before the account's management is formally transferred to the child. This glitch can be easily avoided by simply naming a custodian who is not also the donor. That can be the child's parents or a trusted friend or adviser. There is no requirement that the person who opens the account also must manage it.

Using an UGMA to Emancipate

One New York tax accountant has another idea for high-income parents who have the wherewithal and desire to transfer significant assets to their children. Use an UGMA to "emancipate" your minor, providing him with enough money to pay more than 51 percent of his own expenses. That gives him the ability to claim income-tested education tax credits that you simply can't touch.

You can do this in one of two ways: You can transfer appreciated assets as Junior needs them, being careful to stay below the $11,000 annual estate-tax exemption. (Each individual may give any recipient up to $11,000 per year, without estate- or gift-tax consequences. That means a husband and wife can give $22,000 annually to one child tax free.)

For instance, if the child needs $20,000 in his first year of college to pay room, board, transportation, and other expenses, Mom and Dad may transfer over $20,000 of the GE stock that they bought for a song back in 1970. They would transfer the shares directly into their son's account. The son would then be free to sell the shares as he needed the money.

By transferring the shares, rather than cash, Mom and Dad save themselves from having to pay capital gains taxes on the sale. Assuming that $15,000 of the $20,000 was profit, rather than principal, these parents save $3,000 in federal tax.

Doesn't Junior have to pay that tax when he sells? No. Because he is paying his own expenses from his own money, he is no longer a dependent. As an individual taxpayer, his standard deduction rises to $4,700, and he gets a full $3,000 personal exemption credit, too. That reduces the income on which he'll pay tax by $7,700.

He carries over his parents' "basis" or tax cost in the stock, so he'd be claiming $15,000 in capital gains income on the sale. He subtracts the $7,700 from that and finds he has $7,300 in taxable income. If this were ordinary income, that would heap a $1,099 tax bill on Junior. Given that it's capital gains income, he would owe just $730.

Either way, Junior has another tax break to claim. Because he earns less than $41,000, and he's a freshman in college, he can claim the Hope tax credit, which reduces his tax bill by 100 percent of the first $1,000 in college tuition expenses that he pays, and by 50 percent of the next $1,000 of tuition and fee expenses. The bottom line is that if he paid $2,000 on college tuition, his tax bill would be zero, thanks to the credit. (More on tax credits and deductions in Chapter 10.)

The other option: Mom, Dad, and other interested relatives could have funded Junior's college coffers over time, building up a stockpile that was ready and waiting for him to use by the time he hit college age.

Risks

Of course, with the " appreciated asset transfer" approach described above, parents must have a lot of faith in Junior. They have to trust that he'll use the money as intended and not to buy a world-class stereo system. Alternatively, when parents transfer the money as they go along, they retain a touch more control. If Junior flunks out of college, for instance, they can stop transferring assets. Even if they opt to transfer the money over time, however, bear in mind they are still putting a fair amount of money aside before they know much about how Junior is going to grow up.

They may enjoy a few more tax breaks with the over-time approach. After all, earnings on the assets in an UGMA account are generally taxed at the child's rate. This is a particular benefit for assets like bonds that might throw off ordinary income, but they can't take the assets back. If Junior grows up to be a jerk, or is simply more interested in girls or cars or drugs than school, Mom and Dad may have funded a host of unwanted activities.

With UGMA accounts, donors must always weigh the benefit of the tax breaks against the real risk of giving a child unrestricted rights to a large sum of money. If you fund an UGMA account, make sure you pay a lot of attention to raising your children with good morals and character. (Actually, do that under any circumstances.

Character will get your child even further than college.) Pay attention to how the child's character is developing before you put a lot of money into an UGMA. Remember, once you transfer money into an UGMA, the money belongs to the child.

chapter 6

Investing the College Dough

FOR SOME PEOPLE, THIS IS THE MOST INTIMIDATING CHAP-
ter of this book. They can handle saving, but, the combination of
Wall Street-speak and the possibility of loss turn them to jelly when
they contemplate having to invest the college money.

Two bits of good news: First, thanks to 529 plans (discussed in
Chapter 4), you don't have to do the day-to-day investing. You can
have a professional handle all the heavy lifting. That doesn't mean
your college fund will never suffer a loss. But if it does, you'll have
someone to blame other than yourself.

The second thing: When you take away the silly jargon and boil
it down to its basic concepts, investing is easy. It's something you
learned when you were at your mother's knee, reading the fables and
fairy tales of childhood. Here's a quick refresher.

The Ant and the Grasshopper

You know the story. An ant and a grasshopper see each other on a sunny day. The ant is working hard, storing up food for the winter. The grasshopper is enjoying the sunshine. There's plenty of time to plan later when the day isn't so sweet, he says.

When the weather becomes unforgiving, the grasshopper searches mightily and in vain for food. The ant is cozy, warm, and well fed, simply because he planned ahead when times were still good.

Emulating the ant by starting early is the most powerful strategy in college finance, ideally when the children are toddlers but certainly long before your needs are imminent. It works for you in two important ways: It gets you in the habit of spending less than you earn, and it allows your money to work as hard as you do.

Consider this: If you start saving $100 per month when your child is born, and you're fortunate enough to earn an average return of about 8 percent on your savings, you'll have a tidy $43,180 seventeen years later when your child is ready to enroll in school. Only about half of that amount was your principal. The $100 monthly contributions that you put in added up to $20,400. The other half of the work was done by compound interest. Because compound interest was working for you, you didn't need to work as hard.

On the other hand, if you suddenly realized you needed $43,170 for college when your child was in junior high school, you'd have less than five years to save. Even if you were lucky enough to earn that 8 percent return, which is less likely with a shorter time period because you're less risk-tolerant, you'd have to save $588 per month. That's roughly $35,000 of your own money to get the same amount.

That's not all. The family who saved $100 per month for seventeen years is now in the habit of living off $100 less. This means that they can now throw that $100 into paying college expenses as they go. Or maybe they simply put it into plane tickets home, phone cards, or some other little luxury that will make it easier when the child has gone to school.

The family that needed to save nearly $600 a month fairly quickly is probably not in the habit of saving. More likely, they deferred some major expenses, such as the purchase of a car, to pile money into the college coffers. Now that they've funded college, they probably need to recover what they lost. Unless they have received big raises and promotions in the interim that made them considerably richer, they probably don't have the continuing ability to set aside the college money. Worse, if the need for college money dawns on them during a time in which they've lost jobs, lost overtime earnings, or had some major expense that they didn't anticipate, they—like the grasshopper—will be left out in the cold.

The moral: Plan ahead. It makes your life easier and your child's college prospects more secure.

The Milkmaid and Her Pail

Patty, the milkmaid, was balancing a pail of milk on her head while walking to market. Daydreaming as she walked, she thought she'd sell the milk and use the proceeds to buy a chicken. That chicken would lay eggs, which she would sell to buy a new dress and bonnet. She'd look so fabulous in the new clothes that her pretty friend, Polly, would become jealous.

"But I don't care," said Patty. "I shall just look at Polly and toss my head like this." There went the milk, the proposed chicken, the unlaid eggs, and the longed-for dress and bonnet.

Does Patty's story tell us to avoid talking to ourselves and gesticulating wildly, particularly when walking alone, since it risks what you're carrying and makes you look like a crazed street person? Um, sure. But the point of this story is really that you shouldn't keep all of your milk in one pail. Or eggs in one basket. Or money in one kind of investment.

Wise investors divvy their money up, investing some in stocks, some in bonds, some in real estate, and some in bank deposits. That protects them from losing it all in one upset. If Patty had learned that lesson, she might be the proud owner of a poultry farm today.

The Tortoise and the Hare

Some people approach investing like they approach a diet or going to the gym. They wake up one day, feeling flabby and committed to change. They decide to solve the problem—today.

So they go nuts. They sweat. They deprive themselves. They work harder and faster at obtaining this goal than they ever have before. But pretty soon, they get tired. They need a break from all that work and deprivation. They nap. They backslide. And often, they never get back on track.

A far wiser course is to simply plod along like the tortoise. Step by step, inch by inch, you get a little closer to your goal. It may not be exciting, but it's not that tiring, either. It's a pace that you can maintain.

In the world of college finance, the tortoise approach is easy. Virtually every 529 plan in the nation offers some type of automatic savings option. All you need to do is figure out how big a step you can handle: $25 a month, $50, or $100. As long as you are meeting the minimum investment requirements of the fund—and many funds do allow contributions as low as $25 a month—it's up to you. If you prefer to invest through a UGMA or a Coverdell account, you can also find banks and investment companies that will happily accept your automatic monthly contributions. Call your favorite mutual fund, investment firm, or bank and ask. Often, contributions are deducted directly from your checking account. You don't have to think about it; you don't have to write a bunch of checks. They'll do it for you. It makes plodding relentlessly toward your goal a cinch.

Little Red Riding Hood

A wise investor was once asked how to make a fortune. His response: "Save a lot of money and don't lose any."

Simplistic? Sure. But also true. The best way to derail a good financial plan is to risk money that you're not prepared to lose. There are lots of ways to do that, but the quickest is to fall for a good line by a friendly wolf.

Wolves come in a wide variety in finance. The only thing that connects them is that they're usually well-dressed, charming, and ever so convincing: "I *know* your grandmother," the wolf might say. "She'd *love* this investment. I put my *own* grandmother into this..."

You're too smart to fall for a line like that? Did you buy any technology stocks, by any chance? Pick up a few shares of Amazon.com, when it was selling for 2,000 times its projected 2005 earnings? Did you think to ask what happens to the stock price if Amazon doesn't hit that 2005 target? Face it. We're all just a little bit vulnerable to the pack of investment wolves roving Wall Street.

But there are others, too. Have you ever been tempted to take a ride on a "guaranteed" investment that pays considerably more than comparable stock- or bond-market investments, for example? Did you ask who was offering the guarantee? Chances are, it was a wolf in a very pretty nightie, one who just happened to have a first-class ticket out of town that he's going to use just as soon as you try to collect on that guarantee.

Then there are wolves who really *do* know your grandmother. They may be a member of your church or an alumni of your school. They offer an investment to you, your family, and all of your friends. You're getting a preferential deal because the promoter knows you. (It may not occur to you until later that the wolf has never invited you to swim in his Olympic-sized pool or ride on his yacht.) You—and your hundred closest friends and acquaintances—are special. You feel good about that. Consider this true story:

The minister of a small evangelical church was offered an investment that allowed him to earn 22 percent on his money—"guaranteed." He jumped at the chance to buy this "complicated insurance product" because the person peddling it was a popular parishioner who said the minister was only getting this deal because the parishioner really wanted to help the church. A few months into it, the minister had such faith in this investment program that he wanted to know if he could tell a few other parishioners. "Sure, a few selected people could get in," the peddler said. And maybe a few more. "Hey, any friend of yours is a friend of mine." Pretty soon, the news was spreading like wildfire. Parishioners begged to be "let in" to this opportunity, like lambs to the slaughter.

Then, one day, the payments stopped. The promoter was arrested. When the deal unraveled, it turned out that money from the new parishioners was paying the "returns" to the old parishioners and feeding this promoter's opulent lifestyle. There was no actual investment. This was a Ponzi scheme and "affinity fraud"—a scheme aimed at members of an affiliated group, such as a church, fraternity, alumni association, or trade group. These cons are particularly effective because, like the minister at the church, the victims become promoters themselves. The actual con man does less of the convincing.

You should check out your investments carefully. If you're offered something so complex you can't understand it, pass. Good investments and real opportunities are easy to understand. And, contrary to popular belief, they're in vast supply. It's only the scams that are incomprehensible. Any time a broker says, "You must act now. This opportunity won't last," think, "good." Then say, "Goodbye, Gracie." The only reason for the rush is to catch you with an open wallet before you have enough time to come to your senses.

The Pied Piper

Here's the movie treatment for the story: The people of Hamlin had rats and couldn't get rid of them. Along came a guy who had a plan. It worked. He wanted to be paid, but the people refused to pay him now that the problem was gone. "No cash?" he cackled. He led away their children. (Movie treatments are always a little more dramatic than the real story.)

Investors who decide they can't or won't select investments on their own need help. There are plenty of financial planners and investment advisers available to provide the service. However, it behooves you to understand how these investment advisers are paid. There are three ways to pay a planner: Commissions, fees, or a combination of both. If you go to a fee-only planner, you will pay up-front for the plan. For a comprehensive plan, it's not unusual to pay $1,000 or more. If the plan is single purpose—aimed at helping you structure your college savings, for example—it may be less. But chances are, it won't be cheap.

Fee-only planners can also manage your assets. If they do, they'll charge an asset-management fee that's likely to amount to 1 percent to 2 percent of the amount you invested. This also is not cheap.

Many people prefer to deal with commission-based planners because it appears that their advice is free. They don't make you write them a check for their services. They simply earn a percentage on whatever they convince you to buy, be that a 529 plan or an insurance policy.

The problem with the commission method of payment is that it can encourage the planner to recommend products that may be less attractive for you, but that pay big commissions to the planner.

For example, if you invest $10,000 in a mutual fund with a 5 percent "load," only $9,500 goes to work for you. Five percent, or $500, goes to pay the planner who sold the investment. Or maybe the 529 plan you invest in pays the broker a fee equivalent to 0.5 percent of your invested assets each year, effectively boosting the annual fees on the fund.

If you desperately needed investment advice, and your planner steered you to the right investments, this may be a bargain, but it's far from free. Consider two comparable investments, one that pays nothing to a broker and one that pays 0.5 percent per year. We'll assume that they earn the same investment return—say, 8 percent annually—and that each investor plops $10,000 in and doesn't invest additional money. The first investor ends up with $38,786. The second investor takes home $35,645. The $3,141 difference is the all-in cost of that niggling 0.5 percent fee.

The moral of this story: Valuable services are never free. Know the price.

Basics

Investing wisely is simple. It should demand about one hour of time when you're getting started and about ten minutes a year after that to tend your investments.

The time-consuming part—the hour it will take you to get started—involves nothing more complex than putting your money in several investment "pails" to prevent the Patty problem. The trick is to pick pails that are well suited to your goals.

How do you do that? When investing for college, there are two ways to go: One is the 529 approach, which can take many of the investment decisions out of your hands; the other is to go it alone. Those who invest in Coverdell or UGMA accounts are going it alone and must mix their own investments.

Both approaches require a basic understanding of so-called "asset allocation," which is Wall Street's fancy way of saying you've got to divvy your money up among different asset classes. That reduces your risk of losing everything in a single upset. And it provides the ability to match your assets with your goals.

There are only five investment pails, all easily identified by what they do for you. Some assets provide safety of principal, others provide continuing income, and still others provide the promise of asset growth. Certain types of assets protect your portfolio from the ravages of inflation, while some investments simply allow you to speculate—in other words, roll the dice to earn huge returns, or lose it all in a heartbeat. Let's look at the one asset category, speculation, that you can do without, before talking about the others at greater length.

The Speculation Bucket

When investing for college—or frankly, for any important goal—it's wise to avoid speculative investments. These investments can soar or crash overnight, leaving your child with either considerably more or considerably less than he needs. Speculative investments include commodities, limited partnerships, viatical settlements, and investments that advertise "guaranteed" rates of return far higher than market rates.

Although stocks are considered "growth" investments, it is also a speculative strategy to invest a significant amount in just one or two companies. Why? It's the equivalent of putting the whole bucket of milk on your head, or all your chips on the number eight at the craps table.

You may have the flattest cranium in America, the one best suited to carrying all your assets without a spill. Or you may have studied the crap tables for years, counting how frequently all the number combinations come up and calculating how frequently they could. But one small rut in the road or one minor miscalculation can send that investment reeling. Just ask the people who had their life savings in Enron, WorldCom, Global Crossing, or any one of a dozen high-flying companies that turned into train wrecks.

For your child's sake, invest. Don't speculate.

Growth Investments

Growth investments boil down to stocks, both international and domestic. Over long periods of time, they offer the most generous rates of return, in the neighborhood of 10 percent, on average, annually.

However, the thing to remember about stock investments is that the returns vary dramatically from day to day and from year to year. Although the market posted double-digit hikes for five years running—37.43 percent in 1995, 23.07 percent in 1996, 33.36 percent in 1997, 28.58 percent in 1998, and 21.04 percent in 1999—stock prices tanked in 2000, 2001, and 2002. Normally, stocks suffer a down year about one-quarter of the time, according to market research and consulting firm Ibbotson Associates in Chicago.

If returns for the entire market seem difficult to call, returns on individual company stocks are even less predictable. Nonetheless, over long periods of time, a diversified portfolio of stocks has returned roughly 10 percent on average. That handily beats the rate of inflation, not to mention the average returns on all other traditional investments.

Translation: Funding short-term goals with a long-term asset, such as a stock portfolio, is a gamble. But, if you have plenty of time until your child goes to college, stocks should be a significant part of your portfolio because they're the investment most likely to beat the rate of inflation by the largest margin, which boosts your long-term buying power.

To reduce your risk a bit when investing in stocks, you need to do two things: Have a long time horizon, such as ten years or more, and buy a broad basket of company shares, representing companies, big, small, and mid-sized in virtually every industry. For a small investor, the need for broad diversification generally spells mutual funds, or 529 plans that invest in mutual funds.

As your child gets older and your college funding goal becomes nearer, you should be shifting money out of stocks into steadier investments, such as those listed below under the headings "income" and "safety." Most 529 plans do this automatically for those who choose the age-based portfolios. In most other instances, you must do it on your own.

Income

Income investments are bonds, notes, preferred stocks, certificates of deposit, and real estate investment trusts (REITs). The unifying factor with everything but the REITs is this: You're lending somebody money, be it the federal government, your state, a company, or

100

a bank. They're paying you back with interest. You generally know both the return and when you'll get your principal back.

Your risk boils down to determining whether the entity that you lent to is creditworthy enough to pay interest as scheduled and give you back your principal on time and in full. The more creditworthy the borrower, the less interest it usually needs to pay. You, however, have lots of security.

With this type of investment, you can make sure that the "loan" matures at the same time as your need for the funds. You have a child going to school in five years? It's not such a bad idea to put an amount equivalent to the first year's college tuition in a certificate of deposit maturing in five years.

You face the biggest risk with bonds when you purchase bonds that mature after your goal needs to be funded. If you need to sell bonds before maturity, you could get less, or more, than your initial investment. Market prices for bonds vary based on interest rates at the time of sale. If market interest rates are lower than the rates paid on your bonds, the bonds will be worth more than the principal value. That's because whoever holds this bond is getting better-than-market rates on their money. They'll pay a premium for that right. If market interest rates have risen since you bought your bonds, however, you may not be able to convince another investor to buy your old, relatively low-paying bonds at principal value. Instead, investors will "discount" your bonds, paying you less than what you paid. If you can wait until the bonds mature, and if the borrower remains creditworthy, you'll get all of your principal back. But if you need to sell early, you're taking a chance.

REITs are a hybrid investment; they function a bit like both a stock and a bond. These are investment pools that buy shopping centers, apartment buildings, medical offices, and the like, charging the tenants rent and passing a pro rata share of those rents on to investors. They trade on major stock exchanges, sometimes for less and sometimes for more than their actual asset value. While they offer no income guarantees, they often pay generous returns. They're a decent choice for at least a small portion of the money you put in income investments.

Safety

Investments that offer safety of your principal are similar to income investments, but they mature much more quickly. Generally, safety investments, such as short-term Treasury bills, checking deposits, money market accounts, and money market mutual funds, don't pay a lot of interest. In fact, the interest rates usually are just a touch higher than the rate of inflation. On the other hand, your money is secure and readily available to address near-term goals. When your child is just a year shy of college, some of your college savings should be sitting in these types of accounts.

Inflation Protection

Inflation hasn't reared its ugly head since the late 1970s, but when it did, it wreaked havoc on many a financial plan. The U.S. Treasury now sells an investment aimed at combating inflation by guaranteeing returns tied to the Consumer Price Index, which is the U.S. gauge of inflation. Inflation-protection bonds can be purchased directly from the Treasury (www.ustreas.gov) or through mutual funds, such as those offered through PIMCO.

There's one other way to combat inflation, at least on a personal basis. Pay off your debts. Obviously, you should never have a balance on a credit card, but it also makes sense where possible to pay off the auto loan and the home loan. That won't stop college from being increasingly expensive. However, it will roll back your personal expenses, which will make college costs, not to mention retirement costs, easier to pay when they come along.

102

Putting Investments Together

A reasonable investment strategy is likely to include some element of all of the four traditional investments named above. The mix will depend on how much risk you are willing to take and the age of your child.

If you would personally be devastated if the money you had saved for college diminished in value, you should have very little in stocks. Stock prices soar and plunge in short periods. If you can handle the volatility, they're for you. If you can't, you'll miss out on the highs, but you'll also miss the heartburn. It's a reasonable trade-off.

Unfortunately, other than that sage advice, there is no simple formula for divvying up college assets. You might opt to put 70 percent of a preteen's assets in stocks and 30 percent in bonds, or 50 percent in stocks and 50 percent in short-term bonds. You might choose a mix of 40 percent stocks, 40 percent bonds, and 20 percent Treasury bills or money market accounts. Or you might choose 25 percent stocks, 25 percent bonds, 25 percent Treasury bills, and 25 percent inflation-protection securities. Any of these formulas could be reasonable, depending on how much you have to save and how you feel about risk. There is no secret formula for doing this "right." Right is a subjective decision that you make alone. If making the investment choices seems unnerving, consider the 529 approach.

The 529 Approach

As you learned in Chapter 4, 529 plans function a bit like 401(k) accounts. Each plan will offer a limited number of investment options. Some allow you to choose the asset allocation mix, such as the percentage of the account that you want in stocks versus bonds, for example. Some do all of the investment mixing for you, based on the age of your child and what you choose to inform the plan about your risk tolerance. Some let you decide whether you want to mix your own assets, or if you want the plan administrator to do it for you.

If you want the 529 manager to mix assets for you, you'll answer some questions, such as, "How do you feel about risk?" Typically, 529 plans offer three risk choices: aggressive, moderate, and conservative. People who say they're aggressive investors will have comparatively more assets in stocks than will those who say they are conservative.

But 529 managers are likely to put some stocks in virtually every account—and some bonds and some cash in every account—no matter how aggressive or conservative the saver. If the plan uses an age-based approach to mixing assets, as most do, your child's investment mix will gradually become more conservative as she gets nearer to college age, no matter how aggressive an investor you say you are. That's as it should be. It reduces your risk of losing significant sums right before you need the money.

Aside from the low-maintenance aspect of the 529 approach, the other benefit to these accounts is diversification. Many 529 plans divvy your investments widely among different types of mutual funds.

Consider the College Savings Plan of Nebraska, which allows parents to choose between an age-based portfolio; a target portfolio, which keeps the asset-allocation mix constant over time; or individual fund portfolios, where you mix the assets yourself.

If you make the lowest-maintenance choice, the age-based portfolio, the manager will also ask you to describe your risk tolerance. If you say you're an aggressive investor, setting aside college funds for a newborn, the plan will put 100 percent of your assets in stocks, at first. But that doesn't mean you'll own just one mutual fund.

This plan actually divvies up your stock portfolio into a mix of 75 percent domestic equities and 25 percent international stocks. Your domestic equity portfolio consists of an S&P 500 index fund, an extended-market index fund, an income and growth fund, an equity growth fund, an equity income fund, and the Janus "Enterprise" fund. The international component of this choice consists of three international mutual funds. That's nine funds in total, and all of them highly regarded. This is a fairly stupendous mixture of investments that you would have a hard time replicating on your own.

Why? The reason is that outside of the 529 structure, most of these funds have minimum investment requirements of at least $2,000 or so per fund. That would require investing roughly $18,000 to get a comparable investment mix. But with this 529 plan, you have no investment minimums. Parents and students are allowed to invest whatever amounts they can afford.

With the Nebraska plan and most others, the asset mix in the portfolio shifts as your child ages. Instead of being composed of all stocks, the mix would shift into 20 percent bonds when your child reaches age 6. At age 11, another 20 percent of the portfolio goes into the bond market. At 16, 60 percent of the aggressive investor's college fund is in bonds, while 40 percent remains in stocks.

What do you have to do? Read the annual investment statements to make sure this fund continues to meet your goals. It's the low-maintenance way to invest for college. Nebraska, of course, isn't the only state with a wonderful investment mix within its 529 plan. Chapter 15 provides Web addresses, phone numbers, and minimum investment requirements for all the various state plans that were available at press time. More plans are becoming available daily, so it makes sense occasionally to check the supersites—the two web-sites that track all the state 529 plans on a day-to-day basis (also in the resource directory). Between the supersites and the Web-based links, where you can view each plan's specific investment options, investing your child's college money should be a cinch.

chapter 7

IDAs:
The Stealth Scholarship

L AWRENCE IRATE RAN OUT OF STUDENT AID A SEMESTER
short of college graduation. But the Newark, California–based
artist had an ace in the hole—a so-called Individual Development
Account, which is a matched savings account for the working poor.

He had set aside $500 from his own wages. A nonprofit commu-
nity organization matched his savings $2 for $1. The resulting $1,500
was exactly the amount he needed to become the first member of his
family to graduate from college.

Individual Development Accounts (IDAs) may be the best-kept
secret in college finance. Specifically geared to low-income students who are working but not making much money, they are the
equivalent of a scholarship that can double, triple, or even septuple
the student's own dedicated college savings. Groups that sponsor
these programs match the prospective student's savings by amounts
ranging from $.50 to $7 on the dollar, according to the Corporation
for Enterprise Development, a Washington, D.C., organization that
promotes the programs. The most common match is $2 for every $1
the student kicks in.

Individual Development Accounts (IDAs)

Maximum contribution —Generally not limited, but programs will match only up to set amounts, frequently about $500 per participant per year.

Tax benefits — None

Limitations —Eligibility will depend on the participant's household income and, sometimes, age.

—Matching contributions can be tapped only for set goals, which usually include financing college (and sometimes high school or trade school) education, buying a home, or financing a small business.

—Participants must complete a financial education course, which usually consists of six to twenty hours of classes on budgeting, saving, insurance, and investing.

Pros —If you find and qualify for one of these programs, the program will match your college savings. The match rate varies by program, however. The most common match is $2 for every $1 you've saved.

Cons —Participants must be working and saving their own money. And they'll have to attend financial education classes. Still, considering that the average IDA requires fewer than twenty hours of class time and may provide $1,000 in matching contributions, the investment in financial education classes nets the learner more than $50 an hour, plus some financial knowledge that he or she may not have had before. Not half bad.

Tricks —Finding an IDA program that will suit you is difficult because there are few national standards.

Traps —Your funds are not actually matched until you reach your savings goal. At that point, the matching funds go directly to the goal, which in this case is the college, not you. The program will write a check to your school, which will credit that amount to the tuition and fees you owe.

Generally speaking, the student needs to do just three things to qualify: Work, save his or her own money, and attend a certain number of financial education courses through the sponsoring IDA program. The program will provide an account, usually through a participating bank or credit union that the participant can use to squirrel away small amounts of money each month. Participants who hit their savings goals can apply their savings—and the match—to the authorized expenditure.

The only real catch to these programs is finding one and determining if you meet the group's qualification rules. That's tricky, because although roughly 400 programs are operating nationwide, there is little that's standard about them.

The Basics

Individual Development Accounts are dedicated, matched savings accounts, similar to 401(k)s. However, instead of being offered by employers, IDAs are generally offered through both public and private community groups that aim to promote education, housing, and enterprise.

Using a patchwork of state, federal, foundation, and private funding, IDA programs usually promise to match every dollar saved by participants at a set rate. As noted above, this rate can vary from $.50 on the dollar to $7 for each $1 that the participant saves. Matching rates may also vary by goal.

Although there are some variations from program to program, authorized savings goals almost always include financing college, trade school or continuing education; financing the purchase of a first home; and creating seed funding for a new business. About half of existing IDA programs also provide matching contributions for home improvement and job training.

The Concept

The birth of IDA programs goes back to *Assets and the Poor: A New American Welfare Policy* (M. E. Sharpe, Inc., 1991), a book written by Washington University professor Michael Sherraden in which he contended that low-income families needed to accumulate assets in order to pull themselves and their offspring out of poverty. Although the government offers some income-maintenance programs, such as unemployment insurance, disability, and Aid to Families with Dependent Children, national policy discourages asset accumulation by denying many welfare benefits to those with more than $1,000 in assets, he asserted. As a result, many low-income families are just one illness, divorce, or accident away from being destitute.

These federal policies also have helped to fuel a vast disparity in wealth accumulation between the rich and poor. Whereas the top 10 percent of wage earners account for 40 percent of the national income, the top 1 percent control 90 percent of the assets, Sherraden said. Accumulating assets often has a dramatically positive impact on both physical and psychological well-being.

Supporters of IDA programs believed that even the poorest citizens would save if they were given some incentive. A group of foundations, helped by a federal grant, put this theory into action by creating the first major national IDA program, called the American Dream Demonstration project, in 1997. This project, like most IDA programs, offered matching contributions for those saving for these specified, near-term goals.

By June 2000, 13 percent of the participants had taken a matched withdrawal—$603 from their own savings, plus about $1,095 in matching contributions. Roughly one-quarter of those withdrawals was used to buy homes, another quarter was used to start small businesses, 21 percent financed post-secondary education, and about 20 percent of participants used the money for home repairs. A little over half of those who had not yet taken a matched withdrawal planned to use their savings to buy a home.

How did participants find the money to save? Most simply spent less. Two-thirds became more careful shoppers, ate out less often, and spent less on leisure. About one-third worked more hours. A fraction—about 10 percent—actually borrowed money to save in the program in order to get the match.

In his 2001 Congressional testimony, Sherraden described the impact of the program, based on the results of a survey of participants.

❑ Roughly 93 percent became more confident about the future.
❑ 84 percent reported they were more economically secure.
❑ 85 percent felt more in control of their lives.
❑ 60 percent became more interested in making educational plans for their children.
❑ And a nearly identical percentage (59 percent) expected to make further educational plans for themselves.

The American Dream Demonstration project officially expired at the end of 2002. However, program officials vowed to continue to offer IDAs through foundation grants and private funding. As described later in the chapter, there may someday be a national IDA program.

Who Qualifies?

The programs generally are offered to participants who are working but poor, as defined below. Although some plans are offered for children, the bulk are geared to low-income adults who aim to save for important, near-term goals.

About 88 percent of participants live in households with income below 200 percent of the poverty level, and some 21 percent live in households with incomes below 50 percent of the federal poverty line, according to a study conducted by the Corporation for Enterprise Development. The average age of IDA participants is 36, but some participants are as young as 13 or as old as 72, according to the CFED study.

However, the precise income levels and age restrictions on participants are set by the sponsoring organization. Some set strict age and income limits; others do not. The most common qualification requirement is that the participant earn less than 200 percent of the federal poverty guideline for his size household or qualify for the Earned Income Tax Credit (EITC), a lucrative tax break for the working poor. However, some programs set their income requirements based on median household wealth in the community where the program is offered.

For instance, ADVOCAP, a community action agency in Fond du Lac, Wisconsin, offers an IDA program that targets individuals whose income is at or below 150 percent of the federal poverty level. Capital Area Asset Building Corp. in Washington, D.C., offers programs for those whose income reaches 200 percent of the federal poverty guidelines. The Community Action Project in Tulsa, Oklahoma, sponsors two programs that follow different eligibility standards—one based on whether the family qualifies for the Earned Income Tax Credit, and another that offers matched savings for those earning less than 150 percent of the federal poverty guideline. The Shorebank Corporation in Chicago sets the income limits based on the area's median income; those earning less than 60 percent of the median can qualify. The Women's Self-Employment Project in Chicago, meanwhile, is open to low-and moderate-income women from Chicago housing projects.

In other words, the standards vary. If you're working but barely making ends meet and aspire to a goal likely to be sponsored by an IDA program, check around for programs in your area. You may or may not qualify, but it's certainly worth the effort to find out. Information on how to go about doing that is described later in this chapter.

The Match

How much can you expect to get in matching contributions, if you qualify for a program? Again, the answer varies. The Community Action Project in Tulsa provides $1 for $1 matching for education, while the Foundation Communities in Austin, Texas, provides $2 for $1 matching for adults and $4 for $1 matching for children. Meanwhile, the Capital Area Asset Building Corporation (CAAB) in Washington, D.C., will match up to $7 for each $1 the participant saves.

Education Requirements

As mentioned earlier, all IDA programs demand that the participant take a certain number of classes (or attend a set number of sessions) on financial basics. These classes, which generally include the basics of budgeting, buying a home, reading a credit report, evaluating insurance needs, and saving, are sometimes geared to the particular goal that the participant is working toward. Sometimes they simply aim to teach the benefits of saving and investing.

For instance, Alternatives Federal Credit Union demands sixteen hours of class and support group sessions; the Bay Area IDA Collaborative in San Francisco requires participants to complete five weeks of weekly classes before even opening an account; Near Eastside Community Federal Credit Union in Indianapolis offers a six-hour course; and Women's Self-Employment project requires that participants attend bimonthly financial education and support meetings throughout the life of the two-year program.

Savings Requirements

While all IDA programs revolve around participants saving their own money, only some programs have set monthly savings requirements. Others allow participants to save whatever they can afford.

Some have a set time frame marking the beginning and the end of the program, such as a two-year savings goal, while others have a loose structure that could have participants in and out in a matter of months or lingering for years.

Must money be saved every month? Not necessarily. A study of

IDA programs indicated that most participants saved an average of $25 a month and got $50 in monthly matching contributions, accumulating roughly $900 annually in net assets. This study also showed that the average participant made a savings deposit in just seven months out of twelve, with the largest deposits made in March, most likely the result of tax refunds.

Finding an IDA Program

You want to apply to the program with the best match and the quickest and easiest financial education courses, right? Unfortunately, it's not that simple. Most of the programs are community-oriented, which means you have to live and/or attend school in the area served to qualify. Unfortunately, not every area has a program.

There are about 400 IDA programs operating nationwide. Some of them serve large geographic areas and entail few restrictions other than income requirements. Others aim to serve specific communities in narrow geographic areas, immigrant populations, youth, women, or … you name it.

The point is that you probably won't be able to shop for the best IDA program. You'll be lucky to find a single program that you can qualify for, much less two or three to choose from. Looking for an IDA is much like looking for a private scholarship or grant. They're around, but you'll have to be dedicated and tenacious to find one.

Most IDA programs voluntarily register with the IDA Network, an online resource aimed at promoting and advertising the programs. Some community groups that register with the IDA Network even provide detailed materials on the program requirements and offerings. But, understand, this makes finding an IDA program possible, not easy.

In some cases, consumers have complained that the listings are old, the requirements have changed, insufficient funding exists for matching programs, or they can't find a program that meets their specific needs. It's possible that although you're a low-income student who could theoretically qualify for an IDA, there simply isn't an IDA available to serve you. Like scholarships, there just are not as many IDA programs as there are qualified candidates.

However, because these programs often can provide generous amounts of free money, it's worth your time to investigate whether you have any programs near you and whether you can qualify, even if it takes several hours and numerous phone calls to find the right match.

The most efficient way to search the IDA Network site (www .idanetwork.org) is to click on State Pages on the left-hand side of the start page and go to your state. That may provide dozens of hits—or none at all. If your answer is none, look under IDA Initiatives to see if there's an IDA that may accept you even though you're not in its region. This search may require patience. Once you get out of the state-by-state search engine, the geographic mix and program requirements vary all over the map.

Pending Legislation

Wish there were more of a national standard for IDA programs, so you could more easily know whether you qualify and where to find one? Join the club. But there's some hope that this might happen in the future.

In 2002 the Senate Finance Committee voted to approve a national IDA program that would create funding for up to 300,000 new IDA accounts in a demonstration project that would last seven years. In addition to the much-needed funding, the law would create national standards, which could make determining whether you qualify for an IDA program far simpler.

For example, under the proposal passed by Senate Finance, individuals who earned up to $18,000 when single, $30,000 as the head of a household, or $38,000 when married and filing a joint tax return, would qualify. These numbers are based on "adjusted gross income." That's income after deducting contributions to tax-deductible retirement and work-based health care accounts. It's a far cleaner standard than those based on "median" income and poverty levels, which vary by household size and can change every year.

As this book went to press, this bill had not passed into law and looked like a relative long shot. But promoters of these plans are not giving up and believe they have the support of both President Bush and many powerful members of Congress. If they're right, the IDA proposal may be revived, so stay tuned.

What's a Poverty Guideline?

The Omnibus Reconciliation Act of 1981 requires the Department of Health and Human Services to create poverty guidelines, which are aimed at determining eligibility for federal programs for the poor. These guidelines, which are based on household size and, to a slight degree, on geography, are updated annually to reflect changes in the cost of living. They are similar, but not identical, to Census Bureau poverty statistics, which have separate age-based poverty thresholds.

Commonly, public service programs will base participant eligibility standards on how the applicant's income relates to the applicable poverty guideline for his household size. For instance, many IDA programs are open to those earning up to 200 percent of the federal poverty guideline that year. In 2002, that guideline for a single-person household in the forty-eight contiguous states was $8,860. That means an IDA allowing income to 200 percent of that guideline would not accept single applicants once their income exceeded $17,720. If the program set its threshold at 150 percent of the poverty guideline, those earning more than $13,290 would be turned away.

Poverty thresholds are higher in Alaska and Hawaii, where the cost of living is greater. The 2002 single-person poverty threshold was $11,080 in Alaska and $10,200 in Hawaii.

Those with larger families can refer to the following chart to determine the appropriate poverty guideline for their family. Remember,

2002 Health and Human Services Poverty Guidelines

Size of Family Unit	48 Contiguous States	Alaska	Hawaii
1	$8,860	$11,080	$10,200
2	$11,940	$14,930	$13,740
3	$15,020	$18,780	$17,280
4	$18,100	$22,630	$20,820
5	$21,180	$26,480	$24,360
6	$24,260	$30,330	$27,900
7	$27,340	$34,180	$31,440
8	$30,420	$38,030	$34,980
For each additional person add:	$3,080	$3,850	$3,540

SOURCE: *FEDERAL REGISTER,* FEBRUARY 14, 2002

if you're calculating eligibility for an IDA program, multiply the threshold listed here by the applicable percentage allowed by the relevant program—often as much as 150 to 200 percent.

Earned Income Tax Credit

As discussed previously, a handful of IDA programs base eligibility requirements on whether the applicant can qualify for the Earned Income Tax Credit, a tax break for the working poor. Eligibility requirements for the EITC are also adjusted for inflation and change each year. The following requirements were current through 2001:

❑ You must have earned income—that's income from a job, rather than from a retirement plan or welfare—during the year.

❑ Your earned income and "modified adjusted gross income"

Applicable Definitions

Modified adjusted gross income generally is the same as adjusted gross income. It includes wages, salaries, tips, investment income, and distributions from pension plans. However, for those running their own businesses or claiming losses from rental properties that they own, there are special rules. These individuals have to add in any losses claimed on these activities.

Qualifying children, for the purpose of the EITC, are your son, daughter, adopted child, grandchild, great-grandchild, step-child, or eligible foster child, who (1) was under age 19 at the end of the tax year or was under age 24 and a full-time student or permanently and totally disabled and (2) lived with you in the United States for more than half of the tax year—or all of the tax year for a foster child.

must be less than $10,710 if you have no children, $28,281 if you have one qualifying child (see definition above), or $32,121 if you have two or more qualifying children.

❏ Your investment income cannot exceed $2,450 annually.

❏ You *may not* qualify if married and filing a separate return.

❏ You *may not* be a qualifying child for another person claiming the EITC if you are claiming it yourself. (This applies to sixteen-year-olds who have children but live with their own parents.)

chapter 8

The Spendthrift Strategy

YOU CAN'T SPEND YOUR WAY TO WEALTH, BUT SOME WILL
tell you that spending money is a good way to save for college.
Why? Reward rebate programs promise rebates that are directed
into college accounts for every dollar spent with certain retailers and
manufacturers.

Upromise, BabyMint, and EdExpress are three companies that
offer something similar to frequent-flier rewards. But instead
of earning free airline tickets and magazine subscriptions, these
rewards programs pay real money into college accounts owned by
the child (or adult) of your choice.

Sure, most of the rewards add up to nickels and dimes. But, like
throwing change in a jar, if you do it long enough and consistently
enough, you'll accumulate real money. Better yet, some of the
rewards are hooked to purchases of everyday items like gasoline and
groceries, so you don't have to go out of your way to start earning
college money. Some big-ticket transactions, such as home sales
and car purchases, are hooked into the plans, too, promising bigger
chunks in college savings.

Loyalty Rewards Programs

Maximum contribution —None. The three national "loyalty" rewards programs— EdExpress, Upromise, and BabyMint—rebate a percentage (1% to 20%) of your purchases with certain retailers and manufacturers into an account to benefit your child.

Tax benefits —None.

—However, as long as the rewards are directed to a 529 plan or Coverdell savings account and are eventually used for college costs, you won't pay tax on the investment income earned in the account.

Limitations —Each program has signed up a different group of merchants and products. These offer varying rebates, depending on what you're buying and when.

—Most programs "sweep" your rebates into the child's college account just once a month or once a quarter. With two of the three, you don't get interest or investment returns on the rewards in the interim.

—Some require that you buy gift certificates or use coupons to get a reward, which requires some planning to get the most bang for your buck.

Pros — If you use these rewards programs right, there's no downside. You get free money for doing nothing more difficult or time-consuming than signing up online.

Cons —You might end up on a bunch of mailing lists.

Tricks —Sign up for all of them—and get one of the credit cards— and you could potentially get rewards from two different loyalty programs for the same purchases.

—Potentially huge rewards for real estate purchases with certain brokers within some programs.

Traps —If you spend more than you would normally to get a reward, you're blowing $1 to save a couple of cents. Also, don't leave a balance on the credit cards, or you'll spend more in interest charges than you'll ever recoup in rewards.

Is it enough to pay for college? In your dreams, buster. Even the most optimistic projections from the companies themselves don't make such ludicrous claims. But used properly, it's free money that you wouldn't have had if you didn't sign up. That makes it difficult to find a good reason not to participate.

"We are not going to pay the entire tuition check through gas purchases and buying Kellogg's cereal," said Jeff Bussgang, cofounder of Brookline, Massachusetts–based Upromise. "But we can supplement your savings with free money from America's best brands."

There's just one big caveat that's of particular concern for people who are easily influenced and not very good at math. You should never, never, *never* buy something that you wouldn't ordinarily buy just to get the rebate. That equates to spending a dollar to get two cents.

But if you're planning to buy a GM car, anyway, signing up with Upromise could add $150 to your college account. You've got to furnish the spare bedroom? If you happen to find the right bed, drapes, and accessories at Domestications.com—a discount furniture company that sells online and through catalogues—buying that $3,000 ensemble will put $240 into Junior's college account, for members of EdExpress. You're signed on with BabyMint? On the same purchase, the reward isn't as lucrative, but it's still a substantial $120.

"I play all the angles," said Jon Lansner, a financial columnist for the California *Orange County Register,* and a father of two. "You go to Ralph's [a regional supermarket]. You don't pay attention. You buy stuff like you always do. Chances are, you've got something that's paying a rebate."

Lansner racked up about $300 in savings in about three months with Upromise. Officials at BabyMint maintain their customers do about the same, generating roughly $50 in rebates each month. EdExpress brags bigger rebate checks, but there's a catch: It's the only company of the three that charges an annual membership fee. The company's president compares the $25 annual service charge to shopping at Costco: The membership costs something, but pays back more.

But we're getting ahead of ourselves. Let's start with the basics.

What's a College Rewards Program?

College rewards programs are similar to frequent-flier rewards programs. They work on two fronts: If you use a cobranded credit card—in this case, a credit card issued by either BabyMint or Upromise—roughly 1 percent of every purchase comes back to you in the form of cash rebates paid either in the form of a check or through an electronic credit deposited directly into a college savings account.

The second way to get rewards is to shop with participating merchants and/or buy rebate-paying products in the program. If you buy the right products, you get rebates that can add from 1 percent to 20 percent of the purchase price. That's on top of any reward you might have earned by using the credit card.

Who Offers Them?

There are currently three national companies offering these accounts: BabyMint, an Atlanta-based firm, which can be contacted at www.babymint.com; Upromise, based in Brookline, Massachusetts, at www.upromise.com; and EdExpress, which is headquartered in the Dallas suburbs and is best reached at www.edexpress.com.

How Do You Sign Up?

In every case, customers register on the Internet by going to the appropriate website and filling out a form. Anyone can register for free at BabyMint or Upromise. As noted, if you want to register with EdExpress, there's an annual fee of $24.95. The fee can be paid up front, or the company will allow you to pay monthly through a deduction from future rebates.

Generally speaking, the registration process requires you to provide your e-mail address, name, address, and a password. There will also be prompts asking whether you want to know about "special offers" that are automatically filled in with your "yes" response. If you don't want your e-mail inundated with advertising, click again for a "no" response. Two of the three sites, EdExpress and Upromise, also ask you to register credit cards and grocery cards with the site. Once you fill in the appropriate information about your credit cards, those sites automatically track your purchases. You don't have to go back to the sites, unless you want to see what's new or check on your account balance.

How the Programs Work

The substance of each program is the same, but the details vary. These details may help you determine which, if any, of the programs are right for you. In some cases, you might decide to sign up for them all.

To understand exactly how each program works—outside of the generalities we've just covered—let's take them one at a time. They're listed here in alphabetical order.

BabyMint

BabyMint is primarily an *online* shopping service. When you want to buy something, you register at the site and then click to the appropriate retailer. Somehow, by having clicked through the BabyMint site, your purchases with participating retailers all register with the system. (Technology is a wonderful thing.) However, you won't get credit for the purchase until thirty to forty-five days later—presumably after your payment has cleared and you've received your stuff.

The company also has agreements with offline retailers and grocery stores, but to use the program at a brick-and-mortar location, you must print out coupons or buy gift certificates.

The coupons, which you can print from your home computer, sometimes offer big savings, such as the recent promotion of $1.25

BabyMint Short Course

Annual fee: None

Rebates: 1 percent to 20 percent

Formula: Online shopping and offline shopping using coupons and gift certificates that you purchased (or printed) while online.

Selling point: Tuition rewards program, which can double the value of rebates for those choosing particular schools.

Counter point: To get rebates at offline retailers, you need coupons or gift certificates. That's less convenient and, if you're not careful, you could pay more to have the certificates shipped to you than you'd get back in rebates.

Caveat: The service's advertised 20 percent rebates are mainly on magazine subscriptions. The rebates awarded on things you buy every day are considerably lower.

---

off a $4 box of Rice Krispies cereal. For gift certificates, you'll have to plan far enough ahead to buy them online and have them shipped to you before you need them as a gift item.

Also, beware the shipping charges, experts note. As of press time, BabyMint's gift certificate and gift card suppliers charged fairly hefty shipping and handling charges for the individual store certificates. For instance, a $50 Gap gift certificate costs $2.95 to ship. That exceeds the 5 percent rebate you'd earn on that purchase by $0.45. BabyMint is working on eliminating the fees, said Bill Koleszar, BabyMint's chief marketing officer.

In the meantime, he has a trick to get around them. Rather than buying individual store gift certificates, go into the site and get a "super certificate," he advises.

This super certificate is redeemable for any of the other gift certificates on the site. So, you could buy a $100 super certificate, which could then be used to pick up five $5 Blockbuster cards, a $25 Borders gift card, and a $50 gift certificate for Crate and Barrel. There's no shipping and handling charge when you buy the super certificate, he says. Meanwhile, the $100 in shopping nets your child's college fund $5 in rebates.

BabyMint Partners

Some of the major retailers participating in the BabyMint gift certificate program are Old Navy, Banana Republic, J. Crew, Gap, Bed Bath & Beyond, Bombay Company, Crate and Barrel, Illuminations, Restoration Hardware, Borders Books and Music, Sam Goody, Barnes & Noble, Brookstone, The Sharper Image, Saks Fifth Avenue, Petco, Ace Hardware, T.J. Maxx, and Bloomingdale's.

Additionally, Benihana, Rainforest Café, and Red Lobster restaurants sell rebate-producing gift certificates through BabyMint, as do some theatre chains.

Tuition Rewards Colleges

At the moment, BabyMint's biggest selling point is something called its "tuition rewards" program. This program doubles the value of your BabyMint savings with scholarships or tuition discounts at participating colleges. If your child has a BabyMint account worth $300 and wants to attend one of the participating colleges, that college will match the $300. Generally, that's done simply by cutting the school's tuition rate by $300 or by providing a school-funded scholarship. Either way, the net result is that instead of having $300 in savings, you get a $600 value. The other two college rebate programs don't currently have a matching contribution program. But the services are hotly competitive, so they may decide to offer the benefit down the road.

Of course, this benefit does nothing unless your child wants to attend one of the colleges that participate in the program. As this book went to press, there were just 150 tuition rewards schools in twenty-nine states, but the company hopes to sign on at least 350 more. Currently, all of the program's schools are private. If you think your child may be a good candidate for any of the participating institutions, you might consider signing up for BabyMint. After all, registration is free.

The current tuition rewards schools, listed by state, can be found in the resource directory in Chapter 15, pages 253–258.

Guarantees

Is there any way to guarantee that your child's chosen college will still be a part of the "tuition rewards" program a decade from now, when the child is ready for school? No.

One of the many reasons not to change your spending patterns to participate in these programs is that websites are notoriously fickle. You can feel fairly confident that any rebates you've earned and have had deposited into a college fund will be there when your child goes to school. That part of the program is real money, deposited into your beneficiary's account on a regular basis. Money already deposited can't be taken away. However, whether St. Joseph's College in Maine will still be providing matching "tuition rewards" contributions with BabyMint ten years from now when your child enrolls is anyone's guess.

That said, life in general offers few guarantees. As long as you're not giving up something valuable to participate, there's no reason not to take that chance.

EdExpress

EdExpress is the one rebate service for which participants must pay an annual fee. It's like a Costco membership, said president and chief executive Allan Greenly. They make it worth your while, he claims.

EdExpress Short Course

Annual fee: $24.95
Rebates: 1 percent to 30 percent
Formula: Online shopping
Selling point: The rebates are comparatively higher with this service than with either of the other two
Counter point: You have to spend a lot to recover the annual fee and still earn more with this service than you would with the other two.
Caveat: EdExpress may sell your name and shopping habits to other retailers.

Indeed, the $24.95 annual fee is a key to the structure of EdExpress: It allows the company to offer higher rebates, Greenly said. In order to make a profit and pay the rent, the other services "scrape" the manufacturer and retailer rebates that they offer, he notes. In other words, if Crate and Barrel were willing to rebate 8 percent of purchases made through the system, the other two services might take 3 percent of that amount and pass on just 5 percent to the end consumer.

Because EdExpress is paying its rent (and executives) through annual membership fees, it doesn't have to do that. The consumer gets the full rebate. Presumably, anyone who buys a lot gets more that way.

The other point that EdExpress executives like to boast about is that consumers earn interest on their money from the moment the rebate hits their account. With the other services, that doesn't happen as quickly or as often. Instead, BabyMint transfers your rebates once a month to the investment account of your choice, as long as the rebates total $25 or more (the minimum investment requirement for many types of investment accounts). Upromise sweeps rebate money into investment accounts once every three months. If you don't have $25 or more, what you have sits and accumulates and generally gets deposited when it reaches the minimum.

Naturally, when you're talking about interest rates on tiny amounts of savings, the interest is not likely to amount to much. But EdExpress is proud of the distinction and emphasizes that with their program, a third-party financial institution holds the rebate dough. The point: Parents don't have to worry about the solvency of EdExpress. If the company goes bankrupt while holding your child's rebates, a bank will pay those rebates, anyway. This is a good idea. But again, remember that we're not generally talking about life-altering amounts of money.

The most significant differentiating factor between EdExpress and the other two companies is the rebates you get when shopping with participating retailers. EdExpress is not exaggerating when it claims you get more with its program.

Consider: If you buy things from Domestications.com using EdExpress, you receive an 8 percent rebate. If you purchase the same products from Domestications.com through BabyMint, your rebate would be 4 percent.

The Gardener's Supply rebate with EdExpress is 8 percent; with BabyMint, 4 percent. Similarly, the OfficeMax.com rebate with EdExpress is 6 percent; with BabyMint, 3 percent.

How do the EdExpress rebates compare with those offered by Upromise (whose details we'll get to in a minute)? If you order flowers at 1-800-flowers.com through EdExpress, 6 percent of the price goes into your rebate account. If you order through Upromise, it's 3.5 percent.

DisneyStore.com gives you a 5 percent rebate through EdExpress and a 4 percent rebate through Upromise. Lands' End gives a 5 percent rebate through EdExpress, and 3 percent through Upromise. Dell Computer offers a 3 percent rebate through EdExpress, and a 2 percent rebate through Upromise. Hickory Farms' rebate amounts to 7 percent at EdExpress, and 5 percent at Upromise. The accompanying chart summarizes these comparative rates.

Comparison of Rebate Rates
at Selected Retailers

Retailer	BabyMint	EdExpress	Upromise
Domestications.com	4%	8%	4%
Gardener's Supply Company	4%	8%	5%
OfficeMax.com	3%	6%	n/a
1-800-flowers.com	7%	6%	3.5%
DisneyStore.com	3%	5%	4%
Lands' End	3%	5%	3%
Dell Computer	1%	3%	2%
Hickory Farms	4%	7%	5%

The EdExpress Breakeven

For anyone who does a lot of shopping with these participating retailers, the differences can be significant—certainly worth the $24.95 price of admission. If you don't do a lot of shopping, though, the annual fee makes this service less attractive than the others.

Just how much is "a lot" of shopping? It depends on the rebate amounts. The rebates vary by retailer, generally ranging from 1 percent to 8 percent, so you can figure that it takes $312.50 of shopping with an 8 percent rebating retailer to pay the EdExpress annual fee. If your favorite retailers pay just a 1 percent rebate, you have to spend $2,500 to cover the $25 annual fee.

To decide whether to sign up with EdExpress versus one of the free services, contemplate how much richer the rebates are on the products you'd be likely to buy with EdExpress than with one of

Determining the Break-Even Point

JUST HOW MUCH SHOPPING is required to pay back the EdExpress annual fee? Here's a look at the amount of shopping you've got to do just to break even, based on various rebate amounts. If you shop more in any given year, you earn college money. If you don't, you won't.

Rebate Amount	Break-Even Point
1%	$2,500.00
2%	$1,250.00
3%	$833.33
4%	$625.00
5%	$500.00
6%	$416.67
7%	$357.14
8%	$312.50

the free services. That requires a bit of homework—visiting each website and looking at which retailers offer rebates and how much they are.

Generally, as discussed earlier, the EdExpress rebates range from 1 percent to 4 percent richer than the rebates offered by identical retailers on the other sites. Remember that—before the differential puts cash in your college coffers—after paying the EdExpress annual fee, you'll have to spend between $625 and $2,500 *more* with participating retailers. For example, making a $500 purchase with Domestications.com produces an 8 percent, or $40, rebate with EdExpress. After subtracting the $24.95 annual fee, you come out with a net $15.05.

In comparison, Domestications.com would have paid you 4 percent, or $20, had you shopped through BabyMint, and you'd pay no annual fee. Before EdExpress begins to look like a bargain compared to BabyMint, you have to spend more than $625. With retailers such as Hickory Farms, where the differential is just 2 percent between EdExpress and Upromise, for example, you'd have to spend more than $1,250 to make EdExpress the better deal.

Naturally, determining whether you'll spend enough with these companies to recoup the annual fee and make EdExpress worthwhile requires a bit of guessing about how much you'll buy and where. But if you're willing to do the guessing, I'll provide the math. The chart at left shows how much you have to spend to recoup the annual fee, based on rebate amounts ranging from 1 percent to 8 percent. Don't some companies pay even more? Yes, but rarely.

To get rebates with EdExpress, you register your credit cards. Any of your existing credit cards registered with the website will allow you to shop online or offline and still get the college kickbacks.

One More Caution

EdExpress executives say that the other way this company plans to make money is by selling marketing lists. Because EdExpress is able to "aggregate" all your purchases under one umbrella, marketers could get a great picture of what you buy if they purchase your profile from this company. You should realize that you may be putting yourself on a passel of marketing lists by signing up here. If that possibility horrifies you, stick with one of the other services that at least gives you the opportunity to decline the advertising.

Upromise

Upromise is, most likely, the best known of the three college rebate programs. That's partly because the site spends a tidy sum on marketing and partly because the Upromise list of participating retailers is long and includes significant numbers of retailers you see every day.

Upromise Short Course

Annual fee: None

Rebates: 1 percent to 10 percent

Formula: Online or offline shopping, using registered credit cards

Selling point: Upromise has enlisted a vast array of brick-and-mortar retailers, where you can buy everyday items—like groceries and gasoline—and get a college kickback. That makes it easier to get something significant without changing your spending habits.

Counterpoint: The rebates can be lower with Upromise than those offered by the other services.

Caveat: Most rebates are still on brand-name products. If you forego the cheaper generic version just to get the rebate, you'll likely spend more than you'll recover.

It's the one college rebate system that will get you a rebate on gasoline. One penny per gallon goes into the college account if you buy gas through Exxon or Mobil stations, for instance. In addition, an impressive list of grocery stores—Vons, Ralph's, Stop & Shop, A&P, CVS Pharmacies, Winn Dixie, and Star Markets, among others—will also put rebates in your college account if you have registered your grocery cards with Upromise and then use them while buying Kellogg's Cereal, Coca-Cola products, Kleenex, Tide, Tylenol, or Huggies diapers.

Need your transmission repaired at AAMCO? You'll get 5 percent back through Upromise. Sign up for America Online? You get a $50 kickback. Roughly 4 percent of your AT&T long distance bills, and 5 percent of your rental car charges at Avis, get rebated through this service as well. In addition, if you get a home mortgage directly through Countrywide Home Loan, you could receive a $300 kickback. Sell a house with an approved Century 21, Coldwell Banker, or ERA office and you could get up to $3,000 back. (To be specific, the real estate kickback is 0.5 percent of the sale price or $3,000, whichever is less.)

Upromise offers savings on purchases at Borders Books & Music, Circuit City, Osco Drug, Staples, Toys "R" Us, and Waldenbooks. And it has a directory of 7,500 restaurants nationwide where Upromise members can eat and get a rebate on their bill.

How It Works

Signing up for Upromise is free. You simply go online to www.upromise.com and follow the instructions. In this case, in addition to plugging in your name, mailing address, e-mail address, and the name and details about the beneficiary of the college fund, the site will ask you to register your credit cards and grocery cards. By registering your credit cards, whether you shop online or offline, you get credit for purchases with participating retailers and on participating products.

Groceries

As already mentioned, Upromise works with an impressive list of grocery stores. However, you should realize that you are not getting rebates on everything you buy. You get grocery rebates only by purchasing the brand-name products on the Upromise list. Those brand names include Minute Maid, Coca-Cola, Kellogg's cereals, Eggo waffles, Pop-Tarts, Tylenol, Kotex, Old Spice and Olay, Cascade, Tide, Glad bags, and Kleenex, not to mention Welch's jams and jellies and Skippy peanut butter.

It is important, says Ilyce Glink, author of *50 Simple Things You Can Do to Improve Your Personal Finances,* not to change your spending habits to get a rebate. If you buy a more expensive product to get the rebate, you're likely to spend more on the price differential than you get back in rebates. It's far wiser simply to shop carefully, comparing prices as always, and buy what suits your family at the lowest price. If any of those products pay a rebate, great. If they don't, don't worry about it. Your goal is to have the most money at the end of the day to spend or save, as you see fit.

Restaurants

However, if you're dining out, it doesn't hurt to check the Upromise list of restaurants to see if you'd like to eat at a participating restaurant. The restaurant rebates generally amount to 10 percent of the bill, including tax and tip.

To find participating restaurants, go to the Upromise site and click on Find a Restaurant Near You. That will kick back a prompt for your zip code or the city where you'd like to eat. In some cases, there will be literally dozens of restaurants to choose from. In others, there will be few, if any, choices at all. Dine where you wish, but take a moment to investigate.

Shopping

This site's online shopping works much as the other two do. You click through the site to a retailer's website and shop as you normally would. With offline retailers, you need to use the credit cards that you've preregistered with the site in order to receive Upromise rebates. There are a handful of offline retailers that give Upromise rebates on anything you buy. Those stores include Bed Bath & Beyond, Borders Books & Music, Circuit City, CVS Pharmacy, Staples, and Toys "R" Us.

Big-Ticket Items

If you are planning to buy a car, sell a house, or refinance your mortgage, it's wise to check on the Upromise site to get details on how the company's rebates work.

To get the potentially huge real estate kickback, for instance, locate a participating Century 21, Coldwell Banker, or ERA real estate office; not all offices participate. Then mention that you're a Upromise customer before you sign a contract. If your favorite realtor isn't part of the program, ask them to join. Otherwise, you might want to suffer through with someone who is. The minor inconvenience can get you a rebate amounting to 0.5 percent of the home's purchase or sale price, or $3,000, whichever is less. For the math-challenged, that 0.5 percent would net your beneficiary $500 for each $100,000 in sales price.

When buying a GM car, meanwhile, the site suggests that you get the best deal you can. Then come back to the site and type in the "Vin," or Vehicle Identification Number. The kickback is a flat $150.

Caveats

Upromise is the slowest of the three services to send your money off to an investment account, transferring rebates just once every three months. That means that your money isn't earning interest for longer periods, significant if you do one of those big-ticket transactions that nets a big-enough haul to make investment returns matter.

The firm is a registered broker-dealer, however. And it says that account savings are insured by the Securities Industry Protection Corporation. SIPC is the same insurance agency that backs the stocks and bonds you hold in brokerage accounts.

The Shotgun Approach

Is there anything preventing you from signing up for *all* the services, and then using the service that provides the best (or only) rebate with the retailer of your choice? Nope.

In particular, those tempted to sign up for both of the free services—Upromise and BabyMint—really have no compelling reason not to. To get the best rebates this way, you'll need to do a little research when shopping online. But if you have the time to comparison shop for rebates, it could be worth your while. If you're meticulous enough to want to analyze the best service carefully, spend a bit of time at the various college rebate websites guesstimating just how much you'd spend and where. Pay close attention, when doing these comparisons, however. You don't get a rebate on everything you buy at Vons grocery stores with Upromise, for example; you just get rebates when you buy particular merchandise. The sites are not trying to hide the particulars, but the details are sometimes easy to overlook. And oversights can skew your comparisons. In any event, there appears to be nothing stopping you from using a Upromise-registered grocery card and a BabyMint coupon. Nor from registering your BabyMint-branded credit card (see below) with a Upromise retailer. Or vice versa. Can you use Upromise when dining out and BabyMint when shopping online? Sure.

If you like, you can register with all three services and play rebate pinball. But, particularly if you register for EdExpress, make sure you'll do enough shopping on the site to at least break even paying the annual fee.

Upromise and BabyMint "Branded" Credit Cards

Both Upromise and BabyMint issue their own branded credit cards. Like the American and United Airlines frequent-flier cards, every dollar you charge on these cards gets you a 1 percent reward. If you charge with a participating merchant, you get that 1 percent plus the merchant's rebate.

Can you use a BabyMint card with Upromise merchants and get your 1 percent for charging, plus get the Upromise rebate, too, if you're a member of both services? You bet. You could also register either company's branded credit card with EdExpress and get EdExpress rebates coupled with your credit card rebates.

Notably, the credit cards are issued by major financial institutions. Upromise's card is issued by Citibank; BabyMint's card by MBNA. Both Citi and MBNA offer competitive rates, which will vary based on the borrower's credit history. However, the BabyMint card was a slightly better deal at this book's press time. (Such things can change, so make sure you check the terms of the agreement before you sign up.) The best credit risks were being offered a slightly lower annual percentage rate on the BabyMint card than on the Upromise card. With BabyMint there's no annual fee and no cap on the total amount of rebates you can earn in any given year with the charge card, either.

The Upromise card's lowest rate is about 1 percentage point higher than that of the BabyMint card. It currently doesn't charge an annual fee, either, but only $30,000 in charges count toward rebates each year. That means the maximum reward you could earn on charges would be $300 annually. (This $300 annual cap is just on the 1 percent credit card rebate, separate and distinct from the amount of rewards you can earn by shopping with participating merchants. There is no annual limit on how much you can earn through shopping with rebate-generating merchants and with rebate-granting manufacturers.)

One word of warning: It's a great idea to get a Upromise or BabyMint credit card, if you use credit simply for convenience and pay off the balance every month. But as with any credit card, these cards start out with 9 percent interest rates and go considerably higher, depending on market interest rates and your credit rating. If you leave a balance on the card, you will spend considerably more in interest charges than you'll ever get in rebates.

Pay off your credit cards every month. Don't spend more than you can afford. Keeping those two simple rules in mind will do more for your child's college-savings prospects than any amount of spending you can do with any number of rebating merchants and manufacturers.

Passing Money to College Accounts

Generally, when you register with the services, you are asked to register the beneficiary for whom you are saving. If you have already started a college account in that beneficiary's name, you may be able to register that account at the same time and have the rebates sent directly there.

If you have not already established a college account, Upromise is hooked up with 529 plans offered by Fidelity Investments, Salomon Smith Barney, and Vanguard. You can open accounts with these firms, which provide the service with the ability to automatically sweep your rebates into the child's account.

Otherwise, in general, the services allow you to open an account anywhere and have a check mailed to the college account that you designate. In some cases, that will be a 529 plan. In others, it might be a Coverdell account or an UGMA. Both BabyMint and EdExpress allow the rebate checks to be mailed directly to you, as well. In such cases, you don't necessarily need to use the money for college savings.

Tax Implications

Are your rebates taxable? No. The Internal Revenue Service considers these college rebates—and frequent-flier miles, for that matter—to be discounts on the cost of a good or service that you purchased. That makes them nontaxable.

However, if the rebate money goes into a taxable savings account, the investment returns earned on the rebate savings will be taxable. If the money goes directly into a 529 or Coverdell savings account and is eventually used for college costs, even the investment returns on this money will be tax-free forever.

chapter 9

Generous Relatives

I T'S A TOUCHY SUBJECT. AFTER ALL, THIS IS YOUR CHILD. You're committed to the child's support. You don't want to beg for help with college costs, no matter how overwhelming they might seem. Yet, Grandma and Grandpa are flush with cash. They've made it clear that their substantial estate will go to you, your siblings, and your children someday. The trouble is, with college costs what they are, you could really use an advance on that inheritance.

Generous grandparents have been part of the college finance scene since the beginning of time. In fact, so many grandparents have participated in college finance over the years that U.S. tax laws have carved out some special rules to make it easier for them. If your relationship with your family is such that you can broach this subject without alienating your loved ones, there are truly some advantages to having wealthy grandparents provide the inheritance advance that you need.

However, grandparents may not be the only ones who want to help. In many instances, close friends and other members of a family may want to get involved, too. The question is how. By and large, relatives who don't have a lot of cash are often convinced that the amount they can afford to give is too little to matter. This chapter is all about how much of a difference little gifts can make, and how your relatives can structure their largesse to make the most of their generosity, no matter how much is involved.

Grandparent Gifts

Let's first establish clearly that the most important financial goal that grandparents have is their own retirement. They have worked hard all their lives, saved, and acted responsibly. That should ensure that they are able to travel, enjoy hobbies, and live comfortably after their working years are over. If kicking into a child's college account strains the grandparent's lifestyle even slightly, it should be avoided.

There are no student loans to finance retirement. If your child doesn't have enough money to pay for school with cash, she can finance school with debt—student loans are ubiquitous and cheap. (More on those in Chapter 12.) Don't allow yourself, or your child, to ask for help that would harm your parents. Being considerate of your parents' economic well-being is a gift to them that will come back to you someday, when your children have children of their own and are thoughtful enough to look out for your well-being, too.

However, grandparents fortunate enough to have so much income from pensions, Social Security, and investments that they're certain to die eventually with a substantial estate may find that financing college is a great way to do a little inexpensive estate planning. It allows them to get money out of their estate, without any estate- or gift-tax consequences, and into the hands of their heirs. Better yet, distributing at least part of an estate while alive to monitor it provides lots of control over a financial gift without the need for a complicated trust.

About Estate Planning

Who needs to be concerned about estate planning? The question is somewhat complicated, since U.S. tax laws make the answer a moving target. The Economic Growth and Tax Relief Reconciliation Act of 2001 created a stair-step formula for eliminating the estate tax, a long-criticized federal tax that can eat up 55 percent of the value of a large estate.

Specifically, the act raised the tax-free amount U.S. citizens could bequeath to their heirs at death. In 2001 the maximum bequest you could leave tax free was $675,000. In 2002 the threshold rose to $1 million. That threshold remains at $1 million through 2003. It rises to $1.5 million for 2004 and 2005; to $2 million for 2006, 2007, and 2008; and to $3.5 million in 2009. In 2010, the estate tax is repealed: If you die in 2010, no matter how much you leave to heirs, none of it will be subject to estate tax, if current law actually lasts that long.

Now, here's the weird thing: In 2011, the estate tax boomerangs right back to where it is today. Based on current law (Congress changes tax law frequently enough that I feel compelled to throw in that disclaimer), you'll be able to leave your heirs only $1 million in 2011 that would not be subject to estate tax. An estate's value is based on the fair market value of securities and real estate owned at the time of death, plus the value of all personal property.

It's worth mentioning that husbands and wives can leave each other an unlimited amount of money that will not be subject to estate tax. There is a 100 percent marital exclusion from estate tax. However, on the death of the second spouse, estate taxes would be imposed on any estate that exceeds the thresholds mentioned above.

Of course, estate planning would be a cinch if you knew in which year you were going to die. But given that most of us don't have an expiration date, grandparents (or anyone, really) with estates large enough to need some estate planning—but not large enough to need complicated planning—have two very simple options to get out of estate taxes:

141

1 Spend your money, so that you die with no more than the estate-tax exclusion.

2 Give away enough while you're alive to duck under the estate-tax thresholds.

If you choose to give money away while you are alive to anyone but an established charity, you'll have to be concerned with so-called gift taxes. Gift taxes are imposed on any gift worth more than $11,000 annually. You can, however, give as many people as you like $11,000 a year, without incurring estate or gift taxes. If a grandparent wants to give a grandchild more than $11,000 for college in a single year without having to pay gift tax, he can do that, too, provided that certain restrictions are met.

Gifts to a 529 Plan

One option is to help fund a child's college education through what is called a 529 plan (for a detailed description of how these plans work, see Chapter 4). For example, if a grandfather gives money to his grandson through one of these state-sponsored college savings plans, he can essentially make five years' worth of $11,000 annual gifts in a single year. That allows him to fund a 529 plan with $55,000 on the day that the grandson is born, if he likes. The benefit of doing this is that the investment income on that gift is immediately taken out of his estate and placed in the boy's college account.

Investment returns earned within the 529 account are, at worst, tax deferred; at best, they'll be completely tax free. The question of whether they'll be deferred or tax free is a simple one. If the money is actually used to finance college, the investment returns will be tax free. If the grandfather or the grandson pulls the money out for some other purpose, tax will be imposed at the time of withdrawal. A 10 percent federal tax penalty would also be due.

However, if the grandfather is reasonably certain that the money will be used for education (Chapter 4 is replete with good reasons to be fairly sure about this), a $55,000 gift at the grandson's birth could grow to $180,000 by his seventeenth birthday, assuming a 7 percent average annual rate of return. The grandfather would be restricted by estate-tax rules from giving this same child another costly financial gift until the boy's sixth birthday, or five years after he made the $55,000 gift to the 529 plan, whichever comes later. Naturally, he can still recognize birthdays with clothes, toys, and so on, but no big checks.

What happens if the grandfather dies before the five years are up? A portion of the $55,000 could be added back into his estate. If he died three years after funding the 529, for example, $33,000 of the $55,000 gift would have been completed. The other $22,000 would be considered part of his estate, and it would be added to other assets in the estate to determine whether estate taxes would be due. The grandchild still keeps the money. This "add back" is for tax purposes only.

Paying the College

There's another special estate-tax rule for grandparents who don't want to prefund education, but who do want to pay education bills as they arrive. Specifically, if the grandparents make out a check directly to the college or university, they can pay the entire cost of a child's tuition and fees without being subject to estate or gift tax, no matter how large the amount.

Grandparents with lots of money and lots of grandchildren going to costly universities can write as many checks to as many colleges as they like. These gifts, as long as they're paid directly to the college rather than the grandchild, are tax free. Unlike leaving money directly to heirs, giving money this way provides grandparents with lots of control. If they want to impose restrictions for the privilege of attending college tuition free, they could, for instance, make the tuition payment contingent on grades. If the child doesn't maintain a B average, they could pull their support. But for family harmony's sake, grandparents who do plan to attach strings to these gifts would be wise to make those rules clear from the start.

Giving for Gaps

You don't have parents who can actually give $55,000 to each of your kids? Welcome to my world.

Moderate-income grandparents may still be able to help a needy grandchild by helping supplement what she gets through financial aid. With this approach, any dollar they give will probably reduce the amount of debt your child must take on to graduate. Even small gifts can have a big impact.

The process usually works this way: Prospective college students and their parents fill out a financial aid application roughly a year before the child starts college. This application will be sent through a formula that looks at the student's assets and income, the parents' assets and income, and the cost of the college (or colleges) that the student has chosen. Each college that accepts your child will then present her with a financial aid "package." This will include federal scholarships, grants, and aid, as well as state and college-based aid.

Embedded in the formula that produces these aid packages is the thought that the parents and the student should contribute as much as they possibly can before receiving aid. Simply put, the parents and the student will pay until it hurts—sometimes excruciatingly. The government and school will pay after that to ensure that every qualified student is able to obtain a higher education.

Grandparents are not considered in this formula, so any dollar they give their grandchild is subtracted from the amount that she (or you, as the parents) must come up with out of her own pocket. Even if the only help they can provide is $50 or $100 here or there (perhaps replacing birthday or holiday gifts with cash), those are dollars the child probably won't have to borrow. Particularly in the early years of college, when nonsubsidized student loans are left to accumulate compound interest, $100 could be worth more than $125 in foregone debt.

Making the Threshold

You're a high-income professional whose newborns are destined for pricey schools in the future, and you don't need your parents' help? Think again. You might, albeit in a roundabout way. The reason: Your parents can probably meet the income thresholds that allow them to contribute to tax-favored accounts, such as a Coverdell education savings account. But if you earn substantial amounts, you cannot.

Those who earn more than $95,000 when single or $190,000 when married begin to lose their ability to contribute to these accounts. Once single income hits $110,000 and married income hits $220,000, the ability to contribute to Coverdell accounts evaporates completely.

Coverdell accounts are particularly attractive for high-income families who believe their children might want to attend private high schools, as well as private colleges. That's because savings in these accounts accumulate on a tax-deferred basis. Whether the money is used for college, grammar, or high school expenses, it remains tax free when withdrawn. For someone in a high tax bracket, such as those earning more than $100,000, saving in Coverdell accounts can mean literally thousands of dollars in tax savings.

But your mom doesn't have $2,000 to put into a Coverdell account for her wealthy grandson? She would if you gave her $2,000.

The $11,000 annual gift that each person is allowed to give tax free applies to anyone. That means Junior can give his mom and dad money, and they can turn around and give his child money. Isn't that subverting the whole intent of having income restrictions on these savings accounts? Without a doubt. But it's also clear that the tax law does not prevent this in any way.

Indeed, IRS publication 970, "Tax Benefits for Higher Education," explains that "any individual, including the designated beneficiary for whose benefit the account is established, can contribute to a Coverdell" education savings account if the individual's modified adjusted gross income for the year is less than the threshold amounts.

Tax lawyers note that while it is wrong to break the law, there is nothing illegal or immoral about using the loopholes that exist to ensure that you or your family pay the least amount of tax possible.

Affinity Marketing Approach

There's another way that grandparents can help to finance college, without taking any cash out of their pockets. This method involves signing up with a college loyalty program. There are three such programs, and they each allow the participant to get a kickback on everyday purchases which is then placed into his favorite child's college fund. With two of the three programs, there's no fee to join. You simply need to register one or more credit cards with the program. Then, when you buy merchandise with participating retailers, a portion of the purchase price goes into a college account for whatever beneficiary you designate.

Most purchases result in relatively small amounts being added to the fund. However, one of the programs offers rebates on some big-ticket items, such as car purchases and the sale of a home. If your parents are contemplating buying a car or home, and you have any college-bound children in your family, both you and they should consider registering with the program and getting the rebates. It costs nothing, but can potentially generate up to $3,000 in college funds for your favorite beneficiary. For more information on where to sign up and what's involved, see Chapter 8.

Other Options

My niece, Jessica, was the first child in our family. She had two sets of doting grandparents and five sets of aunts and uncles—not to mention close to a stadium-full of extended family and friends, who were almost as excited about the birth of this little miracle as her blood relatives. She was showered with gifts on every occasion, leaving this child with more clothing and toys than she could use in a lifetime.

As an alternative to clothes or toys, I decided to start a college account for her. After all, she wouldn't miss the extra package at Christmas. But it didn't take long to understand why it's far easier to buy gifts: minimum investment requirements.

Nearly all mutual funds require that you invest at least a set amount to open an account. For adult accounts, the investment minimums start at about $2,000. For kids, they're usually set at $500 or so. Naturally, $500 is considerably more than the cost of a dress or a board game. It is, in fact, an amount that's out of reach for most middle-income friends and relatives.

What's the answer? My response was to create something like a pension plan. I put a set amount into an account and allowed Jessica's interest in that account to "vest"—or become hers—over time. Each birthday or holiday, she'd essentially earn more of the account balance. Now that she has reached age 16, the amount I put aside for her as a toddler is all hers.

Other middle-income relatives may want to create an investment pool, instead. In this case, if there were, say, ten relatives who all normally bought $20 gifts for a child on every occasion, these ten folks might decide to cut the value of their physical purchases in half and put the remaining half into an account for the child's benefit. Assuming there are two major gift-giving occasions a year, that would generate $200 annually in cash. In less than three years, this family would have enough to meet minimum investment requirements for many child-oriented mutual funds or 529 plans. If the parents also contribute to the account, the investment minimums would probably be met considerably sooner.

In any event, if these generous relatives stick with the formula and this family is able to earn an average of 6 percent on their money over the course of sixteen years, this child's friends-and-family account will grow to more than $5,000. That may not be enough to get through college, but it certainly gives the child a good start. And it's a gift a child is unlikely to outgrow.

Notably, too, if you've already set up a 529 plan, relatives may be able to contribute small amounts to it. The ability to make occasional contributions to a 529 varies based on the plan. There are more than fifty different state plans to choose from, all with different investment minimums and options. However, anyone contemplating a financial gift for a child with an established 529 plan may want to look at this option before considering others. For more information on 529 plans, see Chapter 4.

Savings Bonds

U.S. savings bonds have always been the perennial favorite for relatives wanting to give a child a financial gift. This is partly because savings bonds are inexpensive and easy to buy.

They come in eight denominations: $50, $75, $100, $200, $500, $1,000, $5,000, and $10,000. They're purchased for half of their face value, so a $50 bond costs $25. However, the bond cannot be redeemed for its face value until it reaches maturity. That maturity date will vary based on the interest rate earned on the bond, but it will never be later than seventeen years following the original issue date.

The bonds can be purchased from virtually any bank, many employers, and directly from the U.S. Treasury. There is never a brokerage or trading fee for purchasing or selling a savings bond.

The interest rate on Series EE Bonds is set every six months at 85 percent of the return set for five-year Treasury bonds at the most recent auction. A newer type of savings bond, the I Bond, is designed to combat the ravages of inflation by offering an interest rate that floats over the consumer price index. Inflation has been low lately, so these bonds don't currently pay huge returns. However, if inflation becomes an issue, as it was in the late '70s and early '80s, these could prove to be great investments.

If savings bonds are not redeemed at the "original maturity" date, which is when the bonds reach their face value, they'll continue to earn interest. Consequently, a $50 bond might someday be worth $100, or even more. However, they stop earning interest thirty years from their original issue date. At that point, it's a mistake not to redeem them. Obviously, you say? About $9 billion in bonds have reached their final maturity and have not been redeemed. Savings bonds are apparently easy to forget.

However, many people buy savings bonds for education because they believe these bonds offer tax benefits. They do, but the tax benefits are not particularly substantial.

Savings bonds, like all bonds issued by the U.S. Treasury, are exempt from state and local taxation. Taxpayers can also defer paying tax on savings-bond interest until the bonds are redeemed. Under the right circumstances, bonds used for higher education may be redeemed tax free. However, those circumstances are fairly rare, particularly when the bonds have been purchased as a gift.

To qualify for the tax-free treatment, the bond must have been purchased after January 1990. The bond's owner must have been at least twenty-four years old on the first day of the month in which the bond was purchased. Translation: To get the tax breaks, the child, who presumably will use the bond someday to finance education, can be named as a beneficiary of the bond, but cannot be the bond's owner.

Proceeds from the bond's sale must be used for "qualified" education expenses. In this case, that's just tuition and fees. Room, board, books, and other college costs do not qualify.

The tax-free treatment is also available only to those earning less than set amounts. These amounts vary from year to year. In 2002, single filers earning less than $57,600 (and meeting the other requirements) could completely exclude interest earned on the bonds from federal tax when using the proceeds to pay college tuition and fees. The tax exclusions begin to phase out once single income exceeds that amount; they're gone completely when a single person earns $72,600 or more. For married couples, the benefits begin to phase out at $86,400 in joint income and are eliminated completely at $116,400. You cannot exclude the income from tax if you're married, filing separately.

For more information about savings bonds, including how to buy them and detailed data on the interest rates, visit the government's savings-bond website at www.savingsbonds.gov. (Be careful in typing the address. If you type in www.savingsbonds.com instead of ".gov," you'll reach a commercial site. This site provides good information about buying and tracking savings bonds, but it is not affiliated with the federal government.)

chapter 10

Tax Breaks for College

I T'S COLLEGE TIME, AND YOU DON'T HAVE ENOUGH SET
aside to pay the whole bill with savings? The good news is that in
the past several years, lawmakers have been practically falling over
each other in a rush to provide tax breaks to parents financing their
children's college bills. That spells both opportunity and stultifying
complexity for parents wanting to take advantage of this largesse.

These college-oriented tax breaks are generous. Some provide
the equivalent of a $1,000 to $1,500 refund of taxes you've already
paid, as a sort of thank-you for being responsible and solvent enough
to pay your child's college bills. But, as with most things related to
tax, there are plenty of limitations, caveats, income restrictions, and
phaseout periods, not to mention tough choices that parents may
have to make between one tax break or another.

Here's a guide to the tax breaks, who can claim them and who
can't, as well as some strategies to qualify when you earn just a touch
too much to claim the most lucrative deductions and credits.

Mind the Tax Consequences
of the Checks You Write

Before getting into the pay-as-you-go tax deductions and credits, it's important to mention that Coverdell accounts and 529 plans (discussed in Chapters 3 and 4, respectively) are tax-favored accounts. You know that. But I mention it again here, because there are restrictions on doubling up on tax breaks. If you are financing *all* of your child's education with assets saved in these accounts, you won't qualify for the pay-as-you-go tax credits and deductions.

Naturally, if you get to the college years and realize that your job is done—you have saved more than enough to cover every bill and every college living expense for every child—you should have few complaints. More likely, however, those college years will arrive and you'll realize that you have *almost* enough. Or, perhaps, you have enough for the first two years, but not enough to finance the bills through graduation. Yet another possibility is that you might have enough for four years of undergraduate expenses, but your little darling explains that she wants to be a doctor. Or a lawyer, psychiatrist, college professor, or some other impressive professional aspiration that will require more schooling and ring up education expenses that you never even contemplated.

In all of these cases, parents would be wise to watch the way they spend their savings. If you coordinate the use of tax-deferred savings and pay-as-you-go tax breaks, you can get considerably more help to cover the costs than if you write checks oblivious to the tax consequences.

Additionally, because ability to claim the breaks often hinges on income, you may want to be careful about who is writing the checks. What tax breaks are available and who can claim them?

152

Hope Tax Credit

College freshmen and sophomores, or the parents who pay their bills, may be able to qualify for the Hope tax credit, a $1,500 tax credit to help recover tuition and fees paid in those first two years of college. The credit equals 100 percent of the first $1,000 in eligible tuition and fees paid in the relevant tax year, plus 50 percent of the next $1,000 in tuition and fees paid with taxable income. *This credit cannot be claimed by those paying college expenses completely with tax-exempt income from a Coverdell or 529 account.* If the child's college *tuition and fees* were 100 percent paid with tax-exempt income from one of these accounts, you lose your ability to claim the Hope tax credit.

What about the room, board, books, and transportation costs that have nearly doubled your child's college costs? These expenses are not covered by the Hope credit. If your child is at least a half-time student, you can pay these bills with your tax-exempt savings, pay the tuition and fees with other out-of-pocket cash (or savings that are in a taxable account), and get tax breaks for both. But if you pay the *tuition and fees* out of a tax-exempt account, you're going to lose either the tax exemption or the tax credit.

Other qualification requirements for the Hope credit:

❑ The student must attend school at least half time and be enrolled in a course of study that would lead to a postsecondary degree or certificate.

❑ A taxpayer's ability to claim this credit is also dependent on income. The credit is available only to those whose "modified adjusted gross income" is less than set amounts.

In this case, "modified" AGI is your adjusted gross income, plus income received from work outside of the United States. (Up to a set amount of income earned from foreign employment usually is exempt from U.S. tax. The theory is that you're probably paying

Applicable Definitions

Adjusted gross income: Income after contributions to work-based retirement and benefit plans are excluded, but before the taxpayer claims any applicable deductions or credits. This figure is reported at the bottom of the first page of the 1040.

Modified adjusted gross income: Adjusted gross income, plus some sources of otherwise nontaxable income. Although modified adjusted gross income is defined differently in different parts of the tax code, when it comes to education tax breaks, it generally equals AGI, plus income earned outside of the United States that would otherwise be nontaxable.

income or sales taxes on that money to your country of residence while living abroad. Taxing that income in the United States would be double-dipping. But ignoring it completely when calculating income-tested tax breaks would unjustly enrich those who earn substantial income abroad, but who claim a low AGI because of foreign-income exemptions.)

The 2003 income thresholds: Taxpayers earning more than $41,000 when single or more than $82,000 when married begin to lose a portion of the Hope tax credit. The credit is completely unavailable to those earning more than $51,000 when single, or $102,000 when married. If your income is between the phaseout thresholds, you calculate your credit by figuring a percentage.

For example, if you are single and earn $45,000, your income is $4,000 over the threshold. The phaseout range is $10,000 for single filers—the difference between the $41,000 income level where the credit begins to phase out and the $51,000 where it's gone completely. You subtract the amount that your income exceeds the threshold from the phaseout range amount ($10,000 minus $4,000) and put the result, $6,000, over $10,000. That equals 0.6, or 60 percent. You can claim 60 percent of the $1,500 credit, or $900.

If you're married, the phaseout range is $20,000. So, if you had modified AGI of $95,000, you'd subtract that from the first income threshold ($81,000) to find that your income exceeds the threshold by $14,000. Subtract that $14,000 from the $20,000 range, and you get $6,000. $6,000 divided by $20,000 is 0.3, or 30 percent. You'd be able to claim 30 percent of the $1,500 credit, or $450.

What if you earn too much to claim any of the credit? You may want to "emancipate" your college student. This wouldn't help your tax situation—indeed, you'd pay more tax because you couldn't even claim the child as a dependent. But the child may be able to get the credit this way. That would reduce your overall family contribution to Uncle Sam, which may be worth considering. But the consequences are serious, so it's not a strategy you should enter into lightly. For a more thorough description of the risks and rewards of emancipating a minor, see page 166 later in this chapter.

Lifetime Learning Credit

The lifetime learning credit is similar to the Hope credit; however, it is not restricted to those in their first two years of college. It can be claimed by those paying for their junior or senior years of college, graduate school, or continuing-education classes. It can also be claimed in lieu of the Hope tax credit for those paying for freshman and sophomore expenses, but this might not be to the taxpayer's advantage.

To calculate the lifetime learning credit, for the 2002 tax year multiply the cost of eligible expenses paid (just tuition and fees), up to $5,000, by 20 percent. That would create a maximum credit amount of $1,000 per year. However, in 2003, the maximum amount of expenses eligible for this credit rises to $10,000, boosting the maximum credit amount to $2,000.

The lifetime learning credit is subject to the same income limitations and phaseout ranges as the Hope tax credit. It also can be applied only to expenses paid for tuition and fees—*not* books, room, board, transportation, insurance, etc.

Hope versus Lifetime

If you qualify for both the Hope and the lifetime learning credit, you'll have to choose between the two. You cannot claim both for the same student. However, you can claim the Hope credit for one child and the lifetime learning credit for another member of your family, who is also ringing up higher-education costs, when applicable.

Assuming you have just one eligible student, the Hope credit had been clearly the better choice through 2002. But with the maximum lifetime learning credit raised to $2,000 beginning in 2003, it may be tougher to make that choice.

What are the considerations?

❏ Total eligible expenses—that's just tuition and fees. (Room, board, books, and transportation costs cannot be used to calculate eligibility for either the Hope credit or for the lifetime learning credit.)

❏ Whether the family has savings to finance the college costs.

❏ Whether that savings is in a taxable account, such as an UGMA, or in a tax-exempt account, such as a Coverdell or 529 plan.

If the family has no tax-exempt savings, they should go for whichever credit will provide them with the highest amount. But remember that the calculation is different for the Hope credit and the lifetime learning credit.

The Hope credit is 100 percent of the first $1,000 and 50 percent of the second $1,000 in eligible expenses. That means a family paying just $2,000 in tuition can claim the full $1,500 Hope credit.

The lifetime learning credit is calculated at 20 percent of eligible expenses. So to claim the full $2,000, a family would have to pay tuition and fees of at least $10,000 annually.

If the family has tax-exempt savings, the calculation of which credit is best becomes even more complex. In many instances, the

Hope tax credit may continue to be the best choice for those who qualify. The reason? The lifetime learning credit uses up a greater amount of "eligible expenses," which have to be paid out of your pocket, rather than from a tax-exempt savings vehicle. You cannot claim tax exemptions and credits for the same costs.

Consequently, a family financing education partly with tax-exempt savings from a Coverdell account (or a 529 plan) may lose the ability to claim either some of the credit or some of the tax exemptions on the withdrawals from the savings account. Lost? This is complicated. An example might help illustrate the point.

Consider two hypothetical families, each earning $80,000 annually. Each family has a college freshman; each has $20,000 saved in Coverdell accounts. Each college freshman goes to a school that charges tuition and fees of $8,000 annually in 2003. Books, transportation, and room and board cost an additional $3,000 annually for total expenses of $11,000 a year. Both college freshmen are full-time students, living at school.

Family #1 opts to claim the Hope tax credit for the child's freshman year. To do that, they must spend at least $2,000 of their own taxable income (or taxable savings) on college costs. Their withdrawals from the Coverdell account cannot exceed $9,000 (the total college expenses are $11,000, minus the $2,000 in eligible expenses that they must use to qualify for the Hope tax credit). They claim a $1,500 Hope credit, which reduces their tax on a dollar-for-dollar basis. And, the entire $9,000 Coverdell withdrawal is tax-free. The tax exemption on the Coverdell withdrawal could save them up to $1,800 in federal income tax, assuming that all of the money would otherwise be subject to a 20 percent capital gains rate. Total estimated tax savings: $3,300.

(The accountants and engineers reading this are sputtering. "The Coverdell savings wouldn't be fully taxable!" they cry. "Some of this money is sure to be principal—not taxed at all." So true. But some might be interest income, normally subject to higher ordinary income tax rates, too. To simplify the example, I skipped the various potential income tax rates, ranging from 0 to 38 percent, and used the number in the middle. While this isn't 100 percent accurate, a

157

better guesstimate would require a huge amount of mental gymnastics and is unlikely to produce a significantly different result.)

Family #2 has the same costs and savings. However, it wants to use the lifetime learning credit, knowing that this credit can reduce their taxes by up to $2,000—rather than that paltry $1,500 provided by the Hope credit.

But here's the catch. Both the Hope tax credit and the lifetime learning credit can be applied only against "eligible" expenses. The only *eligible* expenses for these credits are tuition and fees. Since this hypothetical family has just $8,000 in eligible expenses, the maximum lifetime learning credit would be $1,600—20 percent times $8,000.

That $8,000 cannot come out of tax-exempt savings. So the most this family could take out of the Coverdell account and still preserve the tax-exempt status of the withdrawal is $3,000. Assuming that $3,000 would otherwise be subject to a 20 percent capital-gains rate, preserving the tax exemption on the Coverdell withdrawal would save this family $600 in federal tax.

The bottom line: Although this family would claim an extra $100 in tax credits this way, they'd end up with total tax savings of just $2,200—or $1,100 less than the family who used the Hope tax credit. That's simply because they were allowed to take less from tax-exempt savings.

Moreover, the family using the Hope tax credit probably had an easier time handling cash-flow issues during the student's first years of college, since they were able to take more money out of tax-exempt savings, rather than from their own pockets. Theoretically, at least, Family #1 would have taken $18,000 out of their $20,000 Coverdell account during the student's freshman and sophomore years in college, while Family #2 would have depleted their Coverdell account by just $6,000.

Family #2 has more money to handle for later years of school, you say. Isn't that a good thing? Not necessarily. Savings in a Coverdell account is considered the student's asset in financial-aid calculations, which reduces eligibility for need-based scholarships, grants, and loans.

Consequently, while it's good to have savings, there's no downside to using as much of the savings as necessary in those first few years of college. That's likely to make the student eligible for more aid in his junior and senior years of school, while making the freshman and sophomore years a little easier on Mom and Dad.

Deductions for Higher-Education Expenses

Earn too much to claim either of these tax credits? You may still be able to claim a tax deduction for paying higher-education expenses. Deductions, which simply reduce your taxable income, are not as valuable as tax credits, which reduce your tax on a dollar-for-dollar basis. But they're certainly better than nothing.

In this case, single filers earning no more than $65,000 or married couples earning no more than $130,000 can claim a deduction of up to $3,000 for college tuition and fees paid in 2002. For somebody paying 30 percent of their income in tax, that will save $900. This deduction is a so-called "before the line" break. You do not need to itemize other tax deductions to claim it.

There is no income phaseout for this deduction, says Brenda Schafer, senior tax-research coordinator at H&R Block in Kansas City. This deduction operates on a "cliff" qualification standard: Earn $65,001 as a single filer, and you're no longer eligible.

In addition, the deduction is temporary. The $3,000 student-expense deduction is available in 2002 and 2003; a $4,000 deduction is available in 2004 and 2005. In 2006, this deduction is set to disappear. It's possible that Congress will move to extend or revive it in future years, but as things stand today, your ability to claim the deduction hinges on having qualifying expenses during the four-year deduction window.

Incidentally, the qualification standard changes a bit in 2004 and 2005, too. The basic income thresholds remain the same, but at that point, singles earning up to $80,000 and married couples earning up to $160,000 qualify for partial deductions. In other words, the

Applicable Definitions

Tax credit: Unlike deductions, which reduce taxable income before your total tax obligation is computed, tax credits work more like grocery store coupons. After the taxpayer has calculated how much he owes, he subtracts any applicable tax credits from his final bill. These credits reduce your bill on a dollar-for-dollar basis. However, education tax credits cannot reduce your tax below zero. (Some tax credits, specifically those for low-income taxpayers, can do this, effectively creating a tax subsidy for those who pay no income tax at all.)

Tax deduction: An amount that's subtracted from taxable income. For example, a taxpayer with $60,000 in income and $2,000 in deductions subtracts the $2,000 from the $60,000 before calculating taxable income of $58,000. If you pay 30 percent of your income in federal tax, a $2,000 tax deduction will reduce your tax bill by $600.

break then no longer has a "cliff" eligibility test. Instead, it takes on a complicated phaseout range like the other education tax deductions and credits. This may be an annoyance to taxpayers, but it's keeping a lot of accountants in nice homes and cars.

Expenses qualifying you to take this deduction include tuition, fees, books, supplies, and some other miscellaneous costs that the school says are necessary.

More Choices

What if you're eligible for both the tax credits and the deduction? You can't take both for the same student in the same year. But if you had, say, three students in college in the same year, you could conceivably take the Hope tax credit for one, the lifetime learning credit for another, and the tax deduction for a third.

However, if you have fewer students and have to choose between the deduction and the credit, you'd be wise to calculate your net tax break with both. If your total earnings allow you to slide under all the income thresholds, so that you're not subject to any phaseouts of the deductions or credits, take the credits. They're certain to be more lucrative.

But if you have a high enough income to be faced with the credit phaseouts, you may do better with the deduction. A single filer earning $50,000 would qualify for only 10 percent of the $1,500 Hope tax credit, for example. That would result in a net tax benefit of just $150. This same taxpayer, assuming he pays 25 percent of his income in federal tax, would enjoy a $750 net benefit from the deduction. (That's $3,000 times 25 percent.)

If this single filer earned $46,000, the credit and the deduction would work out to the same amount: $750. If he earned less, the credit would generate a better tax break; if he earned more, the deduction is the better choice.

However, the best choice for you will depend on the year the deduction is claimed, because marginal tax brackets are falling, making deductions comparatively less lucrative over time. It also depends on your personal tax situation. In other words, if you want the best result, you'll have to do the math, using your own filing status and your own income numbers.

Student Loan Interest Deductions

Starting in 2002, interest expenses paid on student loans also became deductible. In previous years, taxpayers were able to take limited deductions for student loan interest payments made during the first sixty months of repayment. The Economic Growth and Tax Relief Reconciliation Act of 2001 eliminated the sixty-month restriction and decreed that up to $2,500 a year in student loan interest expenses is fully deductible.

Restrictions? Sure.

The ability of any taxpayer to claim this deduction depends on how much she earns. The deductions begin to phase out for single filers earning more than $50,000 and married couples with more than $100,000 in joint income. The deductions are eliminated completely once single income exceeds $65,000 and married income exceeds $130,000. Here are some of the key provisions associated with a student loan interest deduction:

❑ To claim the student loan interest deductions, the person paying the loan has to be repaying it for himself, a spouse, or someone who was a dependent at the time the loan was secured.

❑ The loan must be paid in a "reasonable" period of time—a limitation that the IRS doesn't clearly define.

❑ The loan must have been made to pay education expenses for an eligible student. Eligible students must take a course load that qualifies them for at least half-time status.

❑ Deductible interest includes both loan-origination fees and "capitalized" interest. Capitalized interest is defined as interest expenses that accrued while the loan was in deferral and that were later added to the balance of the loan.

❑ The loan does not need to be a federally guaranteed student loan to qualify for the interest deductions. However, it must *not* be a loan from a relative, *nor* a loan from a qualified employer plan, such as a 401(k).

❑ You cannot claim the student loan interest deduction if you are claimed as a dependent on somebody else's tax return.

Coordinating Tax Breaks with Tax-Exempt Savings Plans

In case you have hit your limit of mind-numbing complexity, and thus missed this earlier, it's important to mention again that you cannot double up on tax breaks for the same expenses. If you take an exemption from income by withdrawing money from a Coverdell account or a 529 account, you cannot claim tax credits or tax deductions for the expenses paid with that tax-exempt withdrawal.

But if you have more expenses than withdrawals, you can claim *both* the income exemptions and either the deductions or credits (or all of the above). The pivotal issue is to keep track of how much you're paying for which type of expenses.

As mentioned in the chapters that more thoroughly examine 529 plans and Coverdell accounts, money in these accounts can be used to pay tuition and fees. However, if the student is attending school at least half time, it can also be used to pay room, board, books, and other education-related costs.

This begs a simple strategy for those who have both savings and the ability to meet the income requirements for the tax deductions and credits: Pay the room and board costs with the savings account. Pay tuition and fees with your own cash. That allows you to claim the maximum amount of tax breaks.

How will anyone know which account the money came out of? They won't. In fact, for you, this is a matter of whether to pull a dollar out of your right pocket or your left pocket. You're still out the same dollar. But pull the $1 from the correct pocket—at least on paper—and the government gives you a prize. Congress works in mysterious ways.

What you need to pay attention to are these questions:

❑ How much do you have in total tuition and fee expenses?

❑ How much of those tuition and fees will be "used" by claiming either the Hope tax credit or the lifetime learning credit?

❑ How much in unused tuition and fee expenses, plus other college-related expenses, do you have left? If you withdraw more from tax-exempt savings than the sum here, you'll jeopardize either the tax exemption on your withdrawal or your ability to claim the tax credit.

Making the Income Thresholds

Think you're locked out of the most lucrative education tax breaks because you earn too much? There are two strategies that might help. One works for people who are close to the income thresholds. The other is for very high-income parents who want to combine college planning with estate planning.

Tinkering with Modified Adjusted Gross Income

If your income is within the so-called phaseout ranges for the tax credits, or just slightly above the cliff eligibility standard for the college expense deduction, you may be able to slide under the thresholds by using so-called before-the-line tax deductions.

By and large, these deductions boil down to work-based savings plans, such as 401(k), 403(b), and 457 plans, as well as so-called flexible spending accounts that you may be offered at work. All of these benefit plans allow workers to contribute their own wages to retirement savings plans for their own future benefit—or, in the case of flexible spending accounts, to save for qualified medical expenses or day-care costs that you expect to have in that year.

The amount you contribute to an employee benefit plan, such as a 401(k) or a flexible spending account, will be taken out of your pay before taxes are computed. The Internal Revenue Service acts as if you never earned that money. This both reduces your taxable income in the current year, saving you income taxes, and cuts your adjusted gross income (AGI), which allows you to claim more income-tested tax breaks.

Let's take a look at how it would work for a hypothetical family earning $100,000 a year. This family has a child who just enrolled in college, where tuition and fees amount to $2,000 annually. If this family does nothing to manage their income, they'll lose their ability to claim 90 percent of the Hope tax credit. Their total Hope tax credit is $150, after accounting for the income phaseouts.

But what if they contribute $11,000 to a work-based retirement savings plan? Their taxable income and modified AGI (that's the relevant figure for the Hope credit phaseout) drops to $89,000. Assuming they pay 30 percent of their income in tax, that saves them $3,300. It also allows them to claim more of the Hope tax credit.

Now, their Hope credit amounts to $525. Net federal tax savings: $3,825. (They would probably save more when state income taxes are computed, too.)

You already contribute the maximum amounts to retirement plans? If your company has a flexible health care account, it may be worth considering. Or, if you also have young children who require day care, look into dependent-care accounts, which work much the same way. You set aside your own pretax money to pay the expenses. It reduces your taxable income by a like amount.

Here are some other before-the-line deductions:

❑ Tax-deductible individual retirement account contributions
❑ Archer Medical Savings Account (MSA) deductions (if you have one, you'll know what it is);
❑ Moving expenses
❑ One-half of the self-employment tax
❑ Self-employed health insurance deductions
❑ Simplified Employee Pension Individual Retirement Account (SEP), Savings Incentive Match Plan for Employees of Small Employers Individual Retirement Account (SIMPLE), and other qualified retirement-plan contributions for self-employed individuals
❑ Alimony payments and penalties you might pay for the early withdrawal of savings.

If you are subject to income phaseouts on any of the education tax credits and are not taking advantage of before-the-line deductions, you'd be well advised to seek professional tax advice. A good tax accountant can run a series of projections based on contributing different amounts to these benefit plans. Those projections should help you decide whether to change your current savings strategies or leave them alone.

Emancipating Your Minor

High-income parents who have no hope of managing their income down to the levels required to claim these tax credits may want to take another approach. It combines estate planning with college planning and involves shifting enough income-earnings assets to a college-age child to allow the student to pay his own expenses out of his own money, including whatever wages he earns from part-time work.

What does that do? It causes the child to become a taxpayer rather than a dependent. You lose the dependency deduction for him, but he probably gains a host of deductions on his own return. As a family, you most likely make out by paying less overall to Uncle Sam.

The downside to this approach is that you had better be very certain that your child is able to handle the responsibility of owning his own assets. If he'd be tempted to sell the bonds you transferred into his name to buy a Camaro rather than pay tuition, you'd certainly lose more in assets than you'd ever recover in tax savings.

Moreover, once the money is transferred, it becomes the asset of the child—forever. You don't get to take the money back after he graduates. You don't get to take it back if you don't like his girlfriend or if he fails to complete his education. Like money placed in an UGMA account, any assets you use to emancipate your minor will legally belong to him.

If, after reflecting upon this aspect, you still think your child is highly responsible and you'd like to move some assets from your estate into his hands anyway, discuss this option with a skilled estate planner. If you need a referral, call your state bar association or the American Bar Association at 312-988-5000.

PART THREE

Zeroing in on Financial Aid, Loans, and Scholarships

chapter 11

Financial Aid

I N A PERFECT WORLD, WE WOULD ALL START SAVING FOR our children's college bills from the day they are born. By the time they were grown, ready, and—naturally—eligible for the costly college educations they aspire to, we'd be ready with a pile of cash to pay the bills.

But in the real world, there were diapers and high chairs and tiny cans of formula that cost an arm and a leg. Then there were clothing bills and day care costs and vacations and cars and insurance and housing and the hundred other expenses that make up the years gone by. For many families, having enough disposable income to save substantial amounts for college is a pipe dream.

It's important to mention that if your choices boil down to saving for your own retirement or saving for your child's future college bills, saving for your retirement should win hands down. Financial aid for college students is a good part of the reason why.

In the 2002–2003 academic year, roughly $85 billion in scholarships, grants, loans, and work-study aid was divvied up among some 15 million college students, according to the College Board, the New York–based organization that follows trends in student aid and college pricing. The aid, much of which is financed through your tax dollars, is meant to ensure that every eligible child has the opportunity to attend college.

That's the good news. The bad news is that an increasing share of financial aid for college students comes in the form of loans, rather than outright scholarships and grants. This means that while your child can get through school, she might graduate with loads of debt.

Who Is Eligible for Aid

Generally speaking, you must be a U.S. citizen or a permanent resident to qualify for federal financial aid. You also must have completed high school or obtained a General Education Development Certificate (GED). If you're a man between the ages of 18 and 25, you must register with the Selective Service department, too. (This can be done by checking a box on the financial aid application.)

Naturally, you also must complete a financial aid form and enroll in an eligible education program, which would lead either to a degree or to a certificate of completion. And you must maintain passing grades to continue receiving aid. Incidentally, the better your grades, the more likely you are to get special consideration if you need more aid than what you see on your aid award letter. (Good grades also keep your insurance rates low, so study.)

Determining Need

The ability to qualify for most scholarships, grants, and subsidized loans, the most valuable types of aid, is determined based on economic need. Need is determined by a formula that looks at both the parents' and the student's income and assets. Information about you and your child's income and assets is gathered on a form called the Free Application for Federal Student Aid.

Filling out the FAFSA form is required for anyone who wants any type of student aid—loans, grants, whatever. Those who apply to private colleges may have to fill out a second financial aid form, which could require even more information than the FAFSA. Why? The FAFSA form collects information that's pertinent for the current federal financial aid formulas *only*. Private colleges have their own sources of aid, usually wealthy donors, alumni, and foundations. That aid may be awarded based on the college's own criteria. The aid criteria applied by private colleges is often stricter than the federal formula, which ignores certain types of parental assets.

For instance, federal student-aid formulas do not count money set aside in qualified retirement plans. Even if the parents have millions stored away in 401(k) plans and individual retirement accounts, that money will not figure into the federal aid formula. Home equity is also excluded under current federal financial aid guidelines.

State-sponsored colleges and universities must adhere to the national guidelines. Private colleges, on the other hand, sometimes expect parents to tap into their home equity before they'll provide need-based aid. However, the private college formula may consider special circumstances, such as high medical or dental expenses, that are not factored into the federal aid formula

Start Here

The first step in applying for financial aid is to get a copy of the FAFSA form. Each year the government makes the new forms available in the late fall. These are generally available in high school guidance-counseling and college financial aid offices or from the public library. The Department of Education also allows—indeed, encourages—students and parents to fill out the FAFSA online.

The online application process saves a good ten days in mailing and processing time. However, the FAFSA form is a long, complicated document. It's wise to fill out a hard copy or worksheet before filing it on the Internet, so that you have the necessary information at hand. That will help you file online accurately, and possibly even in one sitting. The online program does allow applicants to save their place and come back to complete the application later, but delay doesn't make the process any easier.

A sample FAFSA form is included at the end of this chapter to help you prepare. This form can't be submitted, but you can use it as a worksheet before filling out the official version.

File Carefully

Take your time reading the instructions. The FAFSA application is confusing, and a slip can cost you dearly. Consider question 47: "As of today, what is the net worth of your and your spouse's current investments?"

If you had skipped lightly through the three previous pages of instructions, you might have missed the fact that the definition of "investments" for purposes of this form *excludes* the value of all of your retirement plans—401(k)s, 457s, IRAs, SEP-IRAs, Keoghs, etc.—as well as the value of cash held in savings and checking accounts and the cash value built up in life insurance policies. It also excludes any equity you've built up in pre-paid tuition plans or in your home.

If you included those assets, you hurt yourself, potentially dramatically. Aid officials, working off your form, would be counting exempt assets and likely double-counting the amount of cash you have on hand.

Even if the answer to one of the FAFSA questions seems patently obvious, make sure you've reviewed the instructions for that line. Otherwise, you and the aid authorities could be using different definitions. You may think your definition is the right one—the one that would be in the dictionary. But they're the ones with the money. So humor them.

Filing Online

If you want to fill out and file the FAFSA form online, there are two Web addresses that you'll need: www.fafsa.ed.gov, which is where you'll find the FAFSA form, and www.pin.ed.gov, which is where you go to get a personal identification number. This PIN works as an electronic signature, allowing you to file the form officially without signing your name to it. It also allows you to file and retrieve your FAFSA form if you are not able to complete the application in one sitting.

Private-School Aid

If your child wants to attend a private school, that school would probably require a second financial aid form. The most commonly used is the College Board's "profile" application. This is similar to the FAFSA, but it requires parents to disclose information about assets that the federal government considers exempt. This book does not show a sample of a profile application, because these forms are customized for the colleges that ask for it.

The Process

A few weeks after you submit financial aid forms, you'll get a student-aid report, reiterating the information you've submitted and explaining your expected family contribution.

The expected family contribution is a pivotal number. The simple way of figuring the aid your child will be eligible to receive is to take the total cost of the college—room, board, books, tuition, fees, and incidentals—and subtract the expected family contribution. If the college addresses 100 percent of need, the financial aid award will amount to the result of that equation.

The Student-Aid Report

One of the reasons the student-aid report (SAR) reiterates the information that you provided is that people make mistakes. If you find that your aid report is riddled with errors, you can correct it online on the Department of Education's website (www.fafsa.ed.gov) or you can make corrections by hand and mail it back to the address on the form.

If, on the other hand, the SAR form was correct, but things have changed in the meantime—maybe you lost your job or had huge medical expenses or unexpected home repairs—you can talk to a financial aid counselor about boosting your total aid award.

Aid counselors do have some flexibility. Along with those federal dollars, they distribute privately funded aid as well as college-sponsored aid. Many schools hold a certain amount of money back, figuring that some students will have unexpected economic woes that they'll need to address at the last minute. Good aid officers also approach college administrators and beg for more university support, when they find that qualified students need more help than the college has already provided.

The earlier you discuss your issues with the school's financial aid office, the better: Scholarships and grants—the best type of aid—go fast. If you wait, the counselor may be restricted to offering no more than college loans or work-study awards. Also, have the sense not to whine to aid counselors unless you absolutely need to, particularly in the first year or two of school. If you can afford to make the payments, even if it's a stretch, do it. Save pleas for help for when you really need them. Often, that's junior or senior year, after the student's saving account is exhausted. You don't want to have established a pattern with the aid counselors that would make them less likely to take you seriously.

Understanding Aid Awards

Although you'll know your expected family contribution from the SAR, you won't know the details of the financial aid package until your child is accepted at a college or university. At that point, the college's financial aid office will prepare and present an aid award letter to the student. That aid award letter will probably offer a mixture of aid. Depending on the student's need, it could include a variety of grants and scholarships, or it could amount to nothing more than subsidized loans.

All things being equal, of course, it's better to receive aid that you don't have to pay back than aid that you do. You don't have complete control over what kind of aid you get, of course. But good students have more control than average students do because they're more likely to be accepted at several colleges. Since each college will present the student with its own aid package, filled with federal, state, and college-based aid, the student may be able to negotiate with her favorite college if another school has offered more aid or simply a better mixture.

Colleges do compete for good students. Unfortunately, they don't compete as hard for kids with great grades as they do for star athletes, so it's unlikely that the parents of an "A" student would get a full ride and season tickets to school sporting events from persuading their child to go to College X versus College Y. However, they may be able to talk College X into giving Junior more scholarship money than loans.

Be careful when comparing aid award letters, however. There is no standard format. Some colleges, attempting to compete for students even when they have insufficient funds to address the student's need, put the best face on what they're giving by failing to mention the total cost of college, such as room, board, transportation, and incidentals. Or they may include information about unsubsidized loans, which are technically not aid. That can be misleading.

If you have lots of award letters and are confused by it all, you can go to the College Board's website to compare what you've been offered on an apples-to-apples basis. To go to the aid-comparison calculator directly, type http://nextstopcollege.cbreston.org/adms/tools/calculator_tool.htm into your browser. Otherwise, you can simply go to the College Board site (www.collegeboard.com) and click on Information for Parents, and then on the prompt for Aid Calculators.

Types of Aid

When it comes to federal student aid, there are seven programs:

❑ **Pell Grants** pay from $400 to $4,000 to eligible students. These grants are paid directly to the college or through the college and do not need to be repaid.

❑ **Federal Supplemental Educational Opportunity Grants** range from $1,000 to $4,000. The grants are paid directly to the college, which disburses the money to the student. The student can transfer the funds back to the college to pay tuition, or can receive a check to pay housing, transportation, or other expenses. SEOG money does not need to be repaid.

❑ **Work-study awards** give you a leg-up for a job on campus, like working at the library or the admissions office. The money you earn is paid to you and does not need to be repaid, just like earnings from any other job. The main difference between work-study jobs and ordinary jobs is that federal rules require that work-study employers pay at least the going minimum wage. Then, too, work-study programs usually put the student in either a job that is pertinent to his major or a cushy job that allows for some study time. Still, cash-strapped students may want to seek higher-paid work elsewhere.

❑ **Perkins loans** are low-interest, fixed-rate loans made to needy students. The maximum amount of Perkins loans for undergraduate students is $4,000 per year; it's $6,000 for graduate students. The money is paid through the school to the student. It must be repaid after the student is in the workforce. But like other student loans, repayment can be deferred if you continue on to graduate school.

❑ **Subsidized Stafford loans** are provided to students with need. In the 2001–2002 academic year, the maximum amounts ranged from $2,625 to $18,500, depending on grade level (freshman, sophomore, and so forth). This loan must be repaid, but the interest that accrues while the student is still in college is paid by the federal government, not the student.

❑ **Unsubsidized Stafford loans** have the same loan limits as subsidized Stafford loans and work largely the same way, with one pivotal difference: The student pays the interest that accumulates during college and after. A student who borrows $2,000 in his freshman year and defers repayment until six months after graduation would have a considerably higher loan balance at graduation, thanks to the interest that's accumulating but not being paid. When the borrower graduates and goes into a repayment period, the interest is usually "capitalized," or added to the balance of the loan.

❑ **Plus loans** are not for the students. The "Plus" in the name stands for parents' loans for undergraduate students. The loan is limited to the cost of the education, minus the financial aid that your child received in that year.

Detailed information about different types of student borrowing is in Chapter 12.

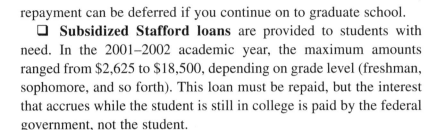

Other Sources of Aid

State governments also offer aid and administer state-federal projects, such as the LEAP (Leveraging Educational Assistance Partnership) program.

State grants and aid generally are included in financial aid offers submitted to students from the various colleges that accept them. However, state education departments can tell you if there are any special scholarships or awards that your child may be able to obtain.

Contact phone numbers for the various state education offices are listed in the financial aid resources section in Chapter 15.

Individual colleges also often have their own sources of aid. These can be private scholarships sponsored by wealthy donors specifically for students who meet atypical criteria—such as being a left-handed tennis player attending Lehigh University—or more general grants and aid that the college simply provides to eligible students.

Private donors also provide a laundry list of scholarships and awards for kids with specific skills, interests, or connections. For more information on these scholarships and awards, see Chapter 13.

A note about these private scholarships: They're counted by the college as aid you have received. That means that scholarships awarded may reduce the aid you get from the government or the college. On the bright side, a private scholarship can replace a loan. While that may not get you more aid dollars, per se, it gives you a better type of aid because it doesn't have to be repaid. And because some colleges can't meet full-need eligibility, private aid is all the more important.

Aid-Boosting Tricks

There are a handful of things that you need to know when applying for aid. The first is that your child's money counts for more than yours in the formula. That's because your child, understandably, has fewer financial obligations than you do. While you will still need to pay the mortgage and the car payment and put food on the table, your child's money is likely to be mainly for education.

Up to 50 percent of the student's income and 35 percent of her assets will be considered "available" to pay college bills *each year.* The amount of *your* income that's considered available to pay college bills each year will vary based on how many children you have, how much you earn, and a variety of other factors. However, *only about 5 percent of your assets* will be figured into the calculation for the estimated family contribution or EFC, which figures prominently in all aid awards.

In dollars and cents, that means $10,000 saved in your child's name will cost her roughly $3,500 in financial aid eligibility each year. That same amount, saved in your name, would cost you about $500 in aid eligibility.

Parents who diligently saved money in Coverdell and UGMA accounts, which are counted as the child's asset, are probably at this moment in the midst of a primal scream. *"Why?"* you moan. *"Why did I save in my child's name?"*

You saved in your child's name because somebody told you it would save money on your income taxes. You probably also thought it was a good idea because it would take some money out of your hot little hands and make it harder to spend. Those were good reasons. But if you have a year or two before your child enrolls in his freshman year of college, you may want to see if you can shift some of those assets out of his name.

Legally, you can't just transfer the money back to yourself. However, you can spend your child's money on him, rather than spending *your* money on him. That reduces the value of his account, while presumably leaving you richer. Maybe you'd planned to buy your sixteen-year-old a car, or to provide him with a down payment for one, so that he could get to and from sports or a part-time job, for example. Instead of you buying the car or putting up the cash for the down payment, take the money out of his UGMA account. This is a perfectly appropriate use of UGMA dollars.

As mentioned in Chapter 5, any expense for the child's benefit, regardless of whether that's for cars or clothing, can come out of UGMA money. At the same time, using this account leaves you free to keep additional money saved in your own name, so that you'll have less trouble financing college bills later.

Spending Down the Coverdell Account

You cannot buy a car with Coverdell dollars without facing tax penalties (see Chapter 3 for details). However, you can pay for private school, tutoring, or related education expenses. For instance, you could buy your daughter a laptop computer and pay for the family's Internet access with Coverdell funds, as long as you can justify that expense as being necessary for school. If your daughter is attending a private high school, the cost of her tuition expenses, books, uniforms, and other school supplies can also be taken out of the Coverdell account.

Naturally, you never want to spend Coverdell or UGMA dollars on something you wouldn't buy otherwise. That simply impoverishes both you and your child. On the other hand, if the expense is necessary, taking it out of the child's account might be aid-wise.

What about 529s?

Under current financial aid formulas, assets held in a 529 account are considered the asset of the donor, not the beneficiary. Because these funds specifically are set up to fund college bills, aid formulas probably will change eventually to acknowledge that this money does belong to the child. However, at the moment, 529 assets are counted as belonging to the parent, not the child. If a grandparent set up the account, these assets might not count in aid formulas at all. But don't get too cozy with that concept because there is some reason behind financial aid formulas. Anything that makes no sense is likely to change.

There is, in fact, serous discussion about changing aid formulas to look beyond whose name assets are held in, thus considering assets as a family rather than by child and then by parent. That would eliminate the jockeying with Coverdell and UGMA accounts and make this whole discussion far simpler. But it hasn't happened yet.

Beware Remarriage

One more warning: Divorced parents should think twice before remarrying if their children are on the brink of enrolling in college. Financial aid formulas look at the new spouse's income and assets, as well as yours, regardless of whether that new spouse is committed to helping you finance college or not. While it's certainly a nice test of your intended's intentions to see if he or she is willing to help support both you and your children, if you're a middle-income family, you might just want to postpone those nuptials until after graduation. Between the marriage penalty in the federal income tax code and financial aid, living in sin is definitely less expensive. (I'm not condoning it, Mom. I'm just stating the facts.)

Setting Up Early

If your child is a decade away from college, you have far greater ability to structure your finances in ways that will help you qualify for federal aid down the road. In a nutshell, these strategies would have you saving prodigiously in exempt asset categories, such as your home and your retirement plans. For details on how to do this, and how it might help you in the future, see Chapter 2.

More Aid Info

The federal government sponsors a terrific financial aid hot line for anyone with questions about financial aid for college. It can be reached at 1-800-4-FED-AID (800-433-3243). The telephone representatives at this number can also provide you with loads of free booklets and information about the various types of financial aid.

If you're wired and Web-literate, there's also a ton of information posted on the Internet. A good place to start is with the Department of Education website at www.ed.gov. There's also www.students.gov, which is another government site aimed at helping students figure out the Byzantine puzzle of federal, state, and private aid. Finally, check out www.finaid.org, a good privately operated website.

Sample FAFSA Form

The FAFSA is the starting point for obtaining all types of government aid—including federally granted student loans. Any family with the slightest chance of obtaining help with college costs should familiarize themselves with the form and procedures for filling it out. Here's a slightly abbreviated sample, provided by the U.S. Department of Education, to help give you an idea of what you're in for.

Parents who will soon need to fill out FAFSA forms can use this sample as a worksheet before attacking the real form online or on paper. If you plan to fill out the FAFSA online, make sure that you get a "PIN number" to sign the form and that you record your password—if not here, somewhere where it can be easily retrieved. If you forget a password after filing a partially completed FAFSA, you can't get it back. You'd have to start over.

FAQs: Before Beginning a FAFSA

What is this application for?
Use this application to apply for federal student grants, work-study money, and loans. You may also use this application to apply for most state and some private aid.

What methods are available for completing the FAFSA?
Several methods are available for completing your Free Application for Federal Student Aid (FAFSA). They are:
- ❏ Paper FAFSA
- ❏ Paper Renewal FAFSA
- ❏ FAFSA on the Web
- ❏ FAFSA on the Web (Spanish Version)
- ❏ Renewal FAFSA on the Web
- ❏ School's system if school participates in Electronic Data Exchange (Contact school for more information)

You may use any one of these methods to apply for federal student aid, but do not submit more than one application.

Also note the following:

❏ If you are filing a **2002 income tax return**, we recommend that you fill it out before completing this form. However, you do not need to send your income tax return to the IRS before you fill out this form.

❏ Transmit no earlier than **January 2, 2003** and no later than **July 1, 2004.**

182

❑ You should receive a SAR within four weeks. If you do not, please refer to the Customer Service page for contact and assistance information to check on the status of your application. For online application status checks, go to www.fafsa.ed.gov and select Check status of a submitted FAFSA, under the FAFSA Follow-up section, 24 hours a day, 7 days a week.

❑ If you or your family have unusual circumstances (such as loss of employment) that might affect your need for student financial aid, check with the financial aid office at the college you plan to attend.

❑ With this form, you may also be able to apply for student aid from other sources, such as your state or college. The deadlines for states or colleges may be as early as January 2003, and may differ. You may be required to complete additional forms. Check with your college's financial aid office for further information on school deadlines.

What records do I need to complete my FAFSA?
In order to successfully complete a FAFSA application, you may need information from one or more of the documents below:
❑ Student's driver's license and Social Security card
❑ W-2 Forms and other records of money earned in 2002
❑ 2002 income tax return (IRS Form 1040, 1040A, 1040EZ; Trust Territory tax return; or foreign country tax return).
❑ Records of untaxed income, such as welfare, Social Security, Aid to Families with Dependent Children (AFDC) or Aid to Dependent Children (ADC), TANF (Temporary Assistance to Needy Families), or veterans benefits
❑ Current bank statements
❑ Current mortgage information for businesses and investments
❑ Business and farm records
❑ Records of stocks, bonds, and other investments
Keep these records! You may need them again. Do not send in your records with your signature page.

What do I need to keep in mind when filling out the FAFSA?
❑ The words "you" and "your" always mean the student. The word "college" means a college, university, graduate or professional school, community college, vocational or technical school, or any other school beyond high school.
❑ Round to the nearest dollar and do not use commas or decimal points.
❑ For dates, type numbers that correspond to the month, day, and year. For example, for November 7, 1974, enter **11071974**.
❑ Questions about your plans and references to the "school year" mean the school year from July 1, 2003 through June 30, 2004.
❑ Do not include notes, tax forms, or letters.
❑ Check with your financial aid administrator if you have unusual circumstances.

How do I know if I am eligible to receive student financial aid?
To be eligible for federal student aid, you must meet certain requirements. You must be:
❑ A U.S. citizen or eligible noncitizen
❑ Registered with Selective Service (if required, see www.sss.gov)
❑ Attending a participating college

❑　Working toward a degree or certificate
❑　Making satisfactory academic progress
Also:
❑　You must not owe a refund on a federal grant or be in default on a federal education loan
❑　You must have financial need (except for unsubsidized Stafford Loans)
❑　You must not have any drug convictions
Other requirements may apply. Contact your financial aid administrator for more information.

What are the deadlines for student financial aid?

College aid deadlines: Colleges may have their own deadlines and applications for awarding student aid. Check with the college's financial aid office for information.

Federal student aid deadlines for the 2003-2004 school year: You should apply as early as possible but not before January 1, 2003. Submitting your form is only the first step in applying for federal student aid. **We must receive your form no later than June 30, 2004.**

State student aid deadlines: State deadlines may be earlier than the federal deadline. Your state may also require an additional form. Check the requirements and deadlines. For more information on these deadlines, see the Deadlines page by selecting the "Deadlines" option from the left navigation bar.

What is the importance of submitting accurate information?

You must fill out this form accurately. The information that you supply can be verified by your college, your state, or by the U.S. Department of Education.

You may be asked to provide U.S. income tax returns and other information. If you cannot or do not provide these records to your college, you may not get federal student aid.

If you get federal student aid based on incorrect information, you will have to pay it back; you may also have to pay fines and fees. If you purposely give false or misleading information on your application, you may be fined $20,000, sent to prison, or both.

Before Beginning a FAFSA Overview: Time Saving Suggestions

Get documents you need: Start with your Social Security Number, driver's license, income tax return, bank statements and investment records.

Print a Pre-Application Worksheet: See a preview of the questions; dependent students can use it to help parents write in info at their convenience.

Plan how to sign your FAFSA: Electronically with a PIN; send a signature page in the mail; or a signed copy of your Student Aid Report.

Speed the process with your PIN: Sign your FAFSA Electronically.

Establish your eligibility: Citizens, non-citizens; with high school diploma or GED; states may use your FAFSA to award additional aid from their programs.

Note important deadlines: We must receive your form no later than June 30, 2003, midnight Central Daylight time. Colleges and states may have earlier deadlines.

FAFSA 2002–2003
Sample from the Online Application

Once you access the form, you may save your application data to our secure database by selecting the Save for Later button at the bottom of each application page. To do so we need the following information. Once this information is entered, you will not be able to change it within the application. If you've entered this information incorrectly, you will need to begin a new application.

A password must be provided and you must remember your password to retrieve your saved application. This is to protect you and your information. A PIN is not the same as the password you have to provide. A PIN serves as your electronic signature and provides access to your other application records such as a "Renewal FAFSA", whereas the password will give you access to a saved but not yet submitted application.

Fill Out Your FAFSA Online

The student's Social Security Number: _____

Please enter this number without the dashes. For example, 123456789.

The student's first two (2) letters of last name: _____

The student's Date of Birth: _____

Please enter this date in "mmdd19yy" format. For example, 08171975.

Create a Password (4 to 8 characters; case sensitive): _____

If you forget your password, you cannot retrieve the FAFSA you saved! Neither Customer Service nor the U.S. Department of Education has a record of your password.

Re-enter the Password: _____

STEP ONE

Step 1 questions relate to your personal demographic and marital status information, as well as school related and financial aid eligibility information that applies to you (the Student).

1. Last Name: _____

2. First Name: _____

3. Middle Initial: _____

4. Permanent Street Address _____

(Include Apt. Number): Only use letters (A-Z), numbers (0-9), periods (.), commas (,), apostrophes ('), dashes (-), number symbols (#), at symbols (@), percent symbols (%), ampersands (&), slashes (/), or blanks (spaces). No other characters are allowed. Use street address abbreviations such as APT (apartment) or AVE (avenue) if the address extends beyond the space provided.

5. City (and Country if not U.S.): _____

6. State: _____

7. Zip Code: _____

8. Your Social Security Number: _____

9. Your date of birth: _____

10. Your permanent telephone number: _____

Please give your telephone area code first. Enter the numbers, without parentheses and dashes. For example, 2025551212.

11. Driver's license number (if any): _____

12. Driver's license state: _____

13. Are you a U.S. Citizen? _____

14. Alien Registration Number: _____

> This question can be left blank if you are an eligible noncitizen only if you selected Canada, Federated states of Micronesia, the Marshall Islands, or Palau as your State of Legal Residence. Your Alien Registration Number can be either 8 or 9 numbers. If your Alien Registration Number is 8 numbers, please enter a zero (0) before your Alien Registration Number.

15. What is your marital status as of today? _____

16. Month and year you were married, separated, divorced, or widowed:

_____

> If divorced, use date of divorce or separation, whichever is earlier. Please enter this date in "mmccyy" format. For example, 081996.

Are you an "early analysis" student? _____

> Answer 'No' to this question if you plan on attending college during the 2002–2003 school year.

(17–21) Choose from Full time/Not sure, 3/4 time, Half time, Less than half time, or Not attending

17. Expected enrollment status for Summer 2002: _____

18. Expected enrollment status for Fall 2002: _____

19. Expected enrollment status for Winter 2002–2003: _____

20. Expected enrollment status for Spring 2003: _____

21. Expected enrollment status for Summer 2003: _____

22. Highest school your father completed: _____

23. Highest school your mother completed: _____

24. What is your state of legal residence: _____

25. Did you become a legal resident of this state before January 1, 1997? _____

26. If the answer to the previous question is "No", give the month and year you became a legal resident: _____

27. Are you a male? _____

(Most male students must register with the Selective Service to get federal aid.)

28. If you are male (age 18–25) and not registered, answer "Yes" and Selective Service will register you. _____

29. What degree or certificate will you be working on during 2002–2003?

_____

30. What will be your grade level when you begin the 2002–2003 school year?

_____

31. Will you have a high school diploma or GED before you enroll? _____

32. Will you have your first bachelor's degree before July 1, 2002? _____

33. In addition to grants, are you interested in student loans (which you must pay back?

_____

34. In addition to grants, are you interested in "work-study" (which you earn through work)?

_____

35. Have you ever been convicted of possessing or selling illegal drugs?

_____

> A federal law suspends federal student aid eligibility for students convicted under federal or state law of possession or sale of drugs (not including alcohol and tobacco). If you answer "Yes" to this question, the Question 35 Worksheet will help you determine whether this law affects your eligibility for federal student aid:

Count only federal or state convictions. Do not count convictions that have been removed from your record. Do not count convictions that occurred before you turned 18, unless you were tried as an adult.

STEP TWO

Step 2 questions relate to your (and your spouse's) income and tax information for the 2001 fiscal year. You do not have to have filed your Income Tax Return Form before filling out this application. However, if you have already completed your 2001 tax form, it will help you complete this section much more accurately and quickly. *Enter whole dollar amounts, and do not use commas.*

36. For 2001, have you (the student) completed your IRS income tax return or another tax return? _____

37. What income tax return did you file or will you file for 2001? _____

38. If you have filed or will file a 1040, were you eligible to file a 1040A or 1040EZ? _____

Select Yes if you (and your spouse) filed or will file a 1040 but were eligible to file a 1040A or 1040EZ. In general, you are eligible to file a 1040A or 1040EZ if you:
Make less than $50,000, do not itemize deductions, do not receive income from your own business or farm, do not receive alimony, and are not required to file Schedule D for capital gains.
Select No if you (and your spouse) filed or will file a 1040 and were not eligible to file a 1040A or 1040EZ.
Select Don't Know if you (and your spouse) filed or will file a 1040 and do not know whether you are eligible to file a 1040A or 1040EZ.

39. What is your (and spouse's) adjusted gross income for 2001? _____
You can find this information on the following tax forms: IRS Form 1040-line 33; 1040A-line 19; 1040EZ-line 4; or Telefile-line I.
If you have not yet completed your 2001 taxes, select the Income Estimator button and answer the questions on the worksheet that is displayed.

40. Enter the total amount of your (and your spouse's) income tax for 2001:

_____

You can find this information on the following tax forms: IRS Form 1040-line 47 + 52; 1040A-line 30 + 34; 1040EZ-line 11; or Telefile-line K(2).

41. Enter your (and your spouse's) exemptions for 2001: _____
You can find this information on the following tax forms: IRS Form 1040-line 6d; 1040A-line 6d or 1040EZ; or Telefile.

42. How much did you earn from working (wages, salaries, tips, etc.) in 2001? Answer this question whether or not you filed a tax return:

_____

You can find this information on the following forms: 2001 W-2 Forms or IRS Form 1040-lines 7 + 12 + 18; 1040A-line 7; or 1040EZ-line 1. Telefilers should use their W-2

43. How much did your spouse earn from working (wages, salaries, tips, etc.) in 2001? Answer this question whether or not your spouse filed a tax return: _____
You can find this information on the following forms: 2001 W-2 Forms or IRS Form 1040-lines 7 + 12 + 18; 1040A-line 7 or 1040EZ-line 1. Telefilers should use their W-2

Worksheet A

For questions that do not apply to you, leave them blank or enter zero.
Did you (the student/spouse) receive any of the following items in 2001?
Items WA1–WA4 are collectively called Worksheet A. The calculated total will be entered automatically on your FAFSA for Question 44.

WA1. Earned income credit from the IRS Form: _____
1040-line 61a; 1040A-line 39a; 1040EZ-line 9a; Telefile-line L(2)

WA2. Additional child tax credit from IRS Form 1040-line 63 or 1040A-line 40:

_____

WA3. Welfare benefits, including Temporary Assistance for Needy Families (TANF). Don't include Food Stamps or subsidized housing: _____

WA4. Social Security benefits received that were not taxed (such as SSI):

_____

44. Total of Student's Worksheet A (WSA): _____
Total of questions WA1–WA4 above. This is a display field only, it holds a running calculation of the entered values.

Worksheet B

For questions that do not apply to you, leave them blank or enter zero. *Enter whole dollar amounts, and do not use commas.*

Did you (the student/spouse) receive any of the following items in 2001?
Items WB1–WB12 are collectively called Worksheet B. The calculated total will be entered automatically on your FAFSA for Question 45.

WB1. Payments to tax-deferred pension and savings plans (paid directly or withheld from earnings), including, but not limited to, amounts reported on the W-2 Form in Boxes 12a through 12d, codes D, E, F, G, H, and S: _____

WB2. IRA deductions and payments to self-employed SEP, SIMPLE and Keogh and other qualified plans from IRS Form 1040-total of lines 23+29 or 1040A-line 16:

_____

WB3. Child support received for all children. Don't include foster care or adoption payments: _____

WB4. Tax exempt interest income from IRS Form 1040-line 8b or 1040A-line 8b:

_____

WB5. Foreign income exclusion from IRS Form 2555-line 43 or 2555EZ-line 18:

_____

WB6. Untaxed portions of IRA distributions from IRS Form 1040-lines (15a minus 15b) or 1040A-lines (11a minus 11b). Exclude rollovers. If negative, enter a zero here: _____

WB7. Untaxed portions of pensions from IRS Form 1040-lines (16a minus 16b) or 1040A-lines (12a minus 12b). Exclude rollovers. If negative, enter a zero here:

_____

WB8. Credit for federal tax on special fuels from IRS Form 4136-line 10 - non-farmers only: _____

WB9. Housing, food, and other living allowances paid to members of the military, clergy, and others (including cash payments and cash value of benefits): _____

WB10. Veterans' non-education benefits such as Disability, Death Pension, or

Dependency & Indemnity Compensation (DIC) and/or VA Educational Work-Study allowances: _____

WB11. Any other untaxed income or benefit not reported elsewhere on Worksheets A and B, such as worker's compensation, untaxed portions of railroad retirement benefits, Black Lung Benefits, disability, etc. Don't include student aid, Workforce Investment Act educational benefits, or benefits from flexible spending arrangements, e.g., cafeteria plans: _____

WB12. Cash received, or any money paid on your behalf, not reported elsewhere on this form: _____

45. Total of Student's Worksheet B (WSB): _____
Total of questions WB1–WB12 above. This is a display field only, it holds a running calculation of the entered values.

Worksheet C

For questions that do not apply to you, leave them blank or enter zero. *Enter whole dollar amounts, and do not use commas.*
Did you (the student/spouse) receive any of the following items in 2001?
Items WC1–WC4 are collectively called Worksheet C. The calculated total will be entered automatically on your FAFSA for Question 46.

WC1. Education credits (Hope and Lifetime Learning tax credits) from IRS Form 1040-line 46 or 1040A-line 29: _____

WC2. Child support paid because of divorce or separation. Don't include support for children in your (the student's) household, as reported in question 84: _____

WC3. Taxable earnings from Federal Work-Study or other need-based /work programs: _____

WC4. Student grant, scholarship, fellowship, and assistantship aid, including AmeriCorps awards, that was reported to the IRS in your (the student's) adjusted gross income: _____

46. Total of Student's Worksheet C (WSC): _____
Total of questions WC1–WC4 above. This is a display field only, it holds a running calculation of the entered values.

47. As of today, what is the net worth of your (and your spouse's) current investments? _____
Net worth means current value minus debt. If net worth is one million or more, enter 999999. If net worth is negative, enter 0.
Investments include real estate (do not include the home you live in), trust funds, money market funds, mutual funds, certificates of deposit, stocks, stock options, bonds, other securities, education IRAs, college savings plans, installment and land sale contracts (including mortgages held), commodities, etc. Investment value includes the market value of those investments as of today. Investment debt means only those debts that are related to the investments.
Investments do not include the home you live in, cash, savings, checking accounts, the value of life insurance and retirement plans (pension funds, annuities, noneducation IRAs, Keogh plans, etc.), or the value of prepaid tuition plans.

48. As of today, what is the net worth of your (and your spouse's) current businesses and/or investment farms? Do not include a farm that you live on and operate.
Net worth means current value minus debt. If net worth is one million or more, enter 999999. If net worth is negative, enter 0.
Business and/or investment farm value includes the market value of land, buildings, machinery,

equipment, inventory, etc. Business and/or investment farm debt means only those debts for which the business or investment farm was used as collateral.

49. As of today, what is your (and your spouse's) total current balance of cash, savings, and checking accounts? (Do not include student financial aid.)

_____

50. If you receive veterans education benefits, for how many months from July 1, 2002, through June 30, 2003, will you receive these benefits? _____
51. What amount of veterans education benefits will you receive per month? (Do not include your spouse's veteran education benefits.): _____

STEP THREE

Step 3 questions determine your dependency status, i.e., whether you are considered a legal dependent to your parent(s), or an independent student. There are a total of seven questions that determine your dependency status. The status dictates whether you need to provide parental data, or if you are exempt from it.

For Step 3, please answer the following questions relating to your dependency status:
52. Were you born before January 1, 1979? _____
53. During the school year 2002–2003, will you be working on a master's or doctorate program (such as an MA, MBA, MD, JD, Ph.D., graduate certificate, or Doctorate of Education, etc.)? _____
54. As of today, are you married? (Answer "Yes" if you are separated, but not divorced.) _____
55. Do you have children who receive more than half of their support from you?

_____

56. Do you have dependents (other than your children or spouse) who live with you and who receive more than half of their support from you, now and through June 30, 2003?

_____

57. Are you an orphan, or are you or were you (until age 18) a ward/dependent of the court? _____
58. Are you a veteran of the U.S. Armed Forces? _____

STEP FOUR

Step Four asks for information about the parents reporting information on this form in reference to the year 2001. This information is required for students considered dependent, and optional for the independent students. A student is identified as being dependent if he/she has answered "No" to every question in Step 3.

Select the "Need help with this page?" link for assistance if you are not sure who should provide parental information in this Step. Your parents do not have to file their Income Tax Return Form before filling out this Step. However, if they have already completed their 2001 tax form, it will help complete this section much more accurately and faster. _Enter whole dollar amounts, and do not use commas._

Other documents that will help your parents are:
Your Parents 2001 W-2 form(s)
Any other of your Parents financial records for 2001
59. What is your parents' marital status as of today? _____

60. What is your father's/stepfather's Social Security Number?

_____

Please enter this number without the dashes. For example, 123456789.

61. What is your father's/stepfather's last name?

_____

62. What is your mother's/stepmother's Social Security Number?

_____

Please enter this number without the dashes. For example, 123456789.

63. What is your mother's/stepmother's last name?

_____

Parents' Household Worksheet

Complete this worksheet to determine who is considered a family member in your parents' household in 2002–2003. The calculated total will be entered on your FAFSA for Question 64.

Your parent(s), or your parent and stepparent, based on their marital status: _____

Yourself (even if you don't live with them): _____

Your parents' other children if: _____

    a. Your parents will provide more than half of their support from July 1, 2002 through June 30, 2003 or **b.** these children could answer "No" to every question in Step 3 (Dependency Status)

Other people if they now live with your parent(s), if your parent(s) will continue to provide more than half of their support, and your parent(s) will continue to provide more than half of their support from July 1, 2002 through June 30, 2003: _____

64. Parent(s) number of family members in 2002–2003? _____

This is a display field only, it holds a running calculation of the entered values.

65. How many in question 64 (exclude your parents) will be college students between July 1, 2002 and June 30, 2003? _____

66. What is your parents' state of legal residence? _____

67. Did your parents become legal residents of the state in question 66 before January 1, 1997? _____

68. If the answer to question 67 is "No," give the month and year legal residency began for the parent who has lived in the state the longest:

_____

69. What is the age of your older Parent? _____

70. For 2001, have your parents completed their IRS income tax return or another tax return? _____

71. What income tax return did your parents file or will they file for 2001?

_____

72. If your parents have filed or will file a 1040, were they eligible to file a 1040A or 1040EZ? _____

Select Yes if your parents filed or will file a 1040 but were eligible to file a 1040A or 1040EZ. In general, they are eligible to file a 1040A or 1040EZ if they: Make less than $50,000, do not itemize deductions, do not receive income from their own business or farm, do not receive alimony, and are not required to file Schedule D for capital gains.

Select No if your parents filed or will file a 1040 and were not eligible to file a 1040A or 1040EZ.

Select Don't Know if your parents filed or will file a 1040 and do not know whether they are eligible to file a 1040A or 1040EZ.

73. What was your parents' adjusted gross income for 2001? _____

You can find this information on the following tax forms: IRS Form 1040-line 33; 1040A-line 19; 1040EZ-line 4; or Telefile-line I.

If your parents have not yet completed their 2001 taxes, select the Income Estimator button and answer the questions on the worksheet that is displayed.

74. Enter the total amount of your parents' income tax for 2001:

_____

You can find this information on the following tax forms: IRS Form 1040-line 47 + 52; 1040A-line 30 + 34; 1040EZ-line 11; or Telefile-line K(2).

75. Enter your parents' exemptions for 2001: _____

You can find this information on the following tax forms: IRS Form 1040-line 6d; 1040A-line 6d or 1040EZ or Telefile.

76. How much did your father earn from working (wages, salaries, tips, etc.) in 2001? Answer this question whether or not your father filed a tax return.

_____

You can find this information on the following forms: 2001 W-2 Forms, or IRS Form 1040-lines 7 + 12 + 18; 1040A-line 7; or 1040EZ-line 1; Telefilers should use their W-2.

77. How much did your mother earn from working (wages, salaries, tips, etc.) in 2001? Answer this question whether or not your mother filed a tax return.

_____

You can find this information on the following forms: 2001 W-2 Forms; or IRS Form 1040-lines 7 + 12 + 18; 1040A-line 7; or 1040EZ-line 1; Telefilers should use their W-2.

Parents' Worksheet A

For questions that do not apply to you, leave them blank or enter zero.

Did your parents receive any of the following items in 2001?

Items WA1–WA4 are collectively called Worksheet A. The calculated total will be entered automatically on your FAFSA for Question 78.

WA1. Earned income credit from the IRS Form: _____

1040-line 61a; 1040A-line 39a; 1040EZ-line 9a; Telefile-line L(2)

WA2. Additional child tax credit from IRS Form 1040-line 63 or 1040A-line 40:

_____

WA3. Welfare benefits, including Temporary Assistance for Needy Families (TANF). Don't include Food Stamps or subsidized housing:

_____

WA4. Social Security benefits received that were not taxed (such as SSI):

_____

78. Total of Parent's Worksheet A (WSA): _____

Total of questions WA1–WA4 above. This is a display field only, it holds a running calculation of the entered values.

Parents' Worksheet B

For questions that do not apply to you, leave them blank or enter zero. *Enter whole dollar amounts, and do not use commas.*

Did your parents receive any of the following items in 2001?

Items WB1–WB11 are collectively called Worksheet B. The calculated total will be entered automatically on your FAFSA for Question 79.

WB1. Payments to tax deferred pension and savings plans (paid directly or withheld from earnings), including but not limited to, amounts reported on the W-2 Form in Boxes 12a through 12d, codes D, E, F, G, H, and S: _____

WB2. IRA deductions and payments to self-employed SEP, SIMPLE and Keogh and other qualified plans from IRS Form 1040-total of lines 23+29 or 1040A-line 16:

_____

WB3. Child support received for all children. Don't include foster care or adoption payments: _____

WB4. Tax exempt interest income from IRS Form 1040-line 8b or 1040A-line 8b:

_____

WB5. Foreign income exclusion from IRS Form 2555-line 43 or 2555EZ-line 18:

_____

WB6. Untaxed portions of IRA distributions from IRS Form 1040-lines (15a minus 15b) or 1040A-lines (11a minus 11b). Exclude rollovers. If negative, enter a zero here:

_____

WB7. Untaxed portions of pensions from IRS Form 1040-lines (16a minus 16b) or 1040A-lines (12a minus 12b). Exclude rollovers. If negative, enter a zero here:

_____

WB8. Credit for federal tax on special fuels from IRS Form 4136-line 10 - non-farmers only: _____

WB9. Housing, food, and other living allowances paid to members of the military, clergy, and others (including cash payments and cash value of benefits):

_____

WB10. Veterans' non-education benefits such as Disability, Death Pension, or Dependency & Indemnity Compensation (DIC) and/or VA Educational Work-Study allowances:

_____

WB11. Any other untaxed income or benefits not reported elsewhere on Worksheets A and B, such as worker's compensation, untaxed portions of railroad retirement benefits, Black Lung Benefits, disability, etc.

Don't include student aid, Workforce Investment Act educational benefits, or benefits from flexible spending arrangements, e.g., cafeteria plans: _____

79. Total of Parent's Worksheet B (WSB): _____

Total of questions WB1–WB11 above. This is a display field only, it holds a running calculation of the entered values.

Parents' Worksheet C

For questions that do not apply to you, leave them blank or enter zero. *Enter whole dollar amounts, and do not use commas.*

Did your parents receive any of the following items in 2001?

Items WC1–WC4 are collectively called Worksheet C. The calculated total will be entered automatically on your FAFSA for Question 80.

WC1. Education credits (Hope and Lifetime Learning tax credits) from IRS Form 1040-line 46 or 1040A-line 29: _____

WC2. Child support paid because of divorce or separation. Don't include support for children in your parents' household, as reported in Question 64: _____

WC3. Taxable earnings from Federal Work-Study or other need-based work programs: _____

WC4. Student grant, scholarship, fellowship, and assistantship aid, including AmeriCorps awards, that was reported to the IRS in your parents' adjusted gross income: _____

80. Total of Parent's Worksheet C (WSC): _____

Total of questions WC1–WC4 above. This is a display field only, it holds a running calculation of the entered values.

81. As of today, what is the net worth of your parents' current investments?

_____

Net worth means current value minus debt. If net worth is one million or more, enter 999999. If net worth is negative, enter 0.

Investments include real estate (do not include the home you live in), trust funds, money market funds, mutual funds, certificates of deposit, stocks, stock options, bonds, other securities, education IRAs, college savings plans, installment and land sale contracts (including mortgages held), commodities, etc.

Investment value includes the market value of those investments as of today. Investment debt means only those debts that are related to the investments.

Investments do not include the home you live in, cash, savings, checking accounts, the value of life insurance and retirement plans (pension funds, annuities, noneducation IRAs, Keogh plans, etc.), or the value of prepaid tuition plans.

82. As of today, what is the net worth of your parents' current businesses and/or investment farms? Do not include a farm that your parents live on and operate.

_____

Net worth means current value minus debt. If net worth is one million or more, enter 999999. If net worth is negative, enter 0.

Business and/or investment farm value includes the market value of land, buildings, machinery, equipment, inventory, etc. Business and/or investment farm debt means only those debts for which the business or investment farm was used as collateral.

83. As of today, what is your parents' total current balance of cash, savings, and checking accounts? _____

NOTE: *Step Five is only completed if you (the student) answered "Yes" to any question in Step Three.*

STEP SIX

In Step Six, you can list up to six colleges, in order of preference, that you would like to receive your 2002–2003 application information (if you are applying to more than six colleges, please select this link to find out what to do). This information also includes the housing plans you have for attending these colleges. You can add or remove any college codes you wish.

Before you begin Step 6, make sure you have the name(s) and address(es) of the college(s) that you would like to receive your 2002–2003 FAFSA results

Which school(s) would you like to receive your 2002-2003 application information? If you are not sure where you will go to college, take your best guess.

If you already know your school's Federal School Code, enter that code in the school code box. When you select the Next button, we will check that code with our database to make sure it is valid.
86. School Code:
Please select your housing plan. Then select Next to enter another Federal School Code or to continue with the application. You can also select Delete This School to remove this Federal School Code.

You have selected the following Federal School Codes and associated housing codes. If you want to add a Federal School Code and associated housing code, select the Add School button. If you want to edit a Federal School Code and its associated housing code, select Edit.

NOTE: You must have at least one Federal School Code entered; you may have up to six.

Sample:

School Code	School Name	Housing Plan
86. 001840	UNIVERSITY OF NOTRE DAME	On Campus

87.
88.
89.
90.
91.

STEP SEVEN

The U.S. Department of Education is required to collect signatures from you and your parents (if applicable) when you file a FAFSA.

There are three ways to sign:
1. Electronically with a PIN
2. By printing, signing and mailing a signature page after you submit an application
3. By signing your SAR and returning it in the mail

NOTES:

If you don't have a PIN, you can print, sign, and mail a signature page when you submit your application. However, the application process is faster if you use your PIN to sign your application electronically.

If you have a current and valid e-mail address (where we can send you instructions on how to retrieve your PIN electronically), you should consider applying for your PIN, as it will speed up your application process. It takes 1–5 days to get a PIN electronically as opposed to the 7–10 days it would take a signature page to be received and processed through the mail. You can use the same PIN throughout your school years for signing your FAFSA application from one year to the next.

You can use your PIN to electronically sign the following application forms:
FAFSA on the Web
Renewal on the Web
Corrections on the Web
Spanish FAFSA on the Web

If you are a dependent student, your parent(s) may also electronically sign your FAFSA using their PIN.

Deadlines

In addition to the federal deadlines for filling out a FAFSA, you may also use the FAFSA to apply for aid from other sources, such as your state or college. The deadlines for states or colleges may differ from the federal deadlines and you may be required to complete additional forms. Check with your high school guidance counselor, state department of education, or targeted school to inquire about their aid deadlines.

Check with your high school guidance counselor or a financial aid administrator at your college about state and college sources of student aid.

Federal Student Financial Aid Deadlines
The 2003-2004 School Year (July 1st, 2003–June 30th, 2004):

FAFSA on the Web, Renewal FAFSA on the Web, and applications must be submitted by midnight Central Daylight time, June 30, 2004.

Corrections on the Web forms must be submitted by midnight Central Daylight time, August 16, 2004.

It is important to note the type of deadline you are up against. Ask your school about their definition of an application deadline, whether it is the receipt date and time or the process date and time of the application. As far as the CPS is concerned, we consider an application's receipt date and time when the application/correction has been successfully submitted. The last page of the online application/correction submission process is therefore called the "Confirmation Page". It contains a 22 (if an application) or 30 (if a correction) character long "Confirmation Number". This number contains the exact date and time (Eastern Standard Time) the form was received. It is recommended you print this for your records.

Note: Transactions must be completed and accepted by midnight to meet the deadline. If transmissions are started before midnight but are not completed until after midnight, those transmissions will not meet the deadline. In addition, any transmission picked up on the deadline date that gets rejected may not be able to be reprocessed because the deadline will have passed by the time the user gets the information notifying him/her of the reject.

FAFSA Follow-Up

Check Status

You can use the application status check to check the status of your FAFSA or correction at any point during the processing period.

Checking the status of your application at any time during the processing period is beneficial, but we recommend you at least check the status at the following times:

1 week after submission: if you used a PIN to sign your application

2–3 weeks after submission: if you printed, signed and mailed a signature page.

Helpful Hint: If you printed out the Electronic Filing Instructions when you filed your Web application, *write down the dates you checked the status.*

chapter 12

Student Loans

FINANCIAL AID FOR COLLEGE STUDENTS IS INCREASINGLY made up of debt. The federal government, state governments, colleges, and universities, as well as a handful of private donors, provide students and their parents with loans to help defray the often overwhelming cost of college.

The Department of Education reports that in 2000, the most recent year for which statistics were available, the average amount borrowed to finance education at a four-year public university was more than $16,000. That's up 35 percent from 1996, when the average debt load of a college senior amounted to just under $12,000. It's not unusual for graduate students to rack up student loans amounting to $50,000, and even $100,000, before they're through.

Consider the story of Nicole Jordan, a law student, who graduated college with $44,000 in student loans. Working through summers and college allowed her to pay off all but $5,000 of her credit card debt. Now she's enrolled in law school and racking up more tuition bills. She estimates she'll add another $50,000 to $60,000 to her debt load by the time she's finished.

The bright side of Jordan's story is that she will complete her education with graduate and undergraduate degrees from respected institutions, despite the fact that her parents were not in a position to help her out financially. And those degrees will probably give her an edge when applying for jobs. Bureau of Labor statistics indicate that the more education you have, the more you are apt to earn and the less likely you are to be unemployed.

According to Census Bureau figures, in 2001, high school graduates earned roughly $27,978 on average, whereas the average earnings of a college graduate were $51,649. Those with master's degrees earned an average of $61,295; those getting a professional degree, like Jordan, earned an average of $95,150. The bottom line: A person with a college degree is expected to earn roughly $1 million more over her lifetime than someone who stopped his education after high school. Those who go on to get a professional degree, such as doctors, lawyers, and engineers, are likely to earn roughly $2 million more than high school graduates, even after accounting for the fact that they'll work fewer years because they're spending more years in school.

All this makes even a $100,000 price tag on college look like a great investment. Therefore, even if you need to take on what seems to be a very large debt load to pay for college, you will probably come out ahead. With that in mind, let's take a look at the whole area of student loans.

Types of Loans

In very simple terms, student loans can be broken into two categories: loans for students and loans for parents. Either type of loan can be made through the Federal Direct Student Loan Program (FDSLP) or the Federal Family Education Loan Program (FFELP).

From the standpoint of interest rates and fees, it doesn't matter whether you get a loan through FDSLP or FFELP—the rules governing how these rates and fees are calculated and charged are identical with both programs. The school that your child attends simply decides to participate in one program or the other.

However, there are two differences between the programs. The first is simply a matter of who is doing the lending. If your school participates in the direct loan program, you don't need to seek a lender. The Department of Education loans you the money.

With FFELP, you'll have to find a bank that makes student loans. Fortunately, that's easy. Financial aid offices often have lists of lenders, with contact numbers and addresses. If the school doesn't have such a list, your state's loan guaranty agency will. The Department of Education has a directory of loan guaranty agencies posted on its website at www.ed.gov/Programs/bastmp/SGA.htm. From there, you can click on the Web link to your state's education department or guaranty association, where you can find more information about aid and lenders.

The second difference between direct loans and FFELP loans is that the direct loan program offers one repayment option not offered through FFELP. This option, income-contingent repayment, is the best choice only for those who leave college for low-paying jobs likely to remain low-paying for exceptionally long stretches. Therefore, for most people, this shouldn't be a significant concern.

However, if you are planning to go into some sort of social work or know that your career goals will probably lead you into a job that will pay poorly for a long period of time, you may eventually want to get your loans transferred into the direct loan program. You can do this regardless of whether your initial loans were made through the direct loan program or FFELP. But it's not something you need to be concerned about until after you graduate college. At that point, look into loan consolidation. (See the section titled "Consolidating Your Loans" later on in this chapter, page 212.)

Who Should Borrow?

If both the student and the parents qualify to borrow money for school, most families should have the student borrow instead of the adults. There are many reasons why:

❑ Student loans are a good way for a young person to establish a credit history. The terms of these loans make it extremely easy to meet the obligations, even under the worst of circumstances. That gives any student who is making an effort the ability to create a pristine credit history that can open the door to low-rate auto financing, low-rate home mortgages, and relatively lower-rate credit cards in the future.

❑ Students do not have to pay back loans while still in school. Parents, on the other hand, generally need to start repaying the debt almost right away.

❑ Students are also more likely to qualify for tax deductions when they begin repaying the loans than would their parents. That's mainly because there are income restrictions governing who qualifies to take advantage of education-related tax breaks. The lower your income, the more likely you are to qualify. (See Chapter 10 for details.)

❑ Finally, there are no "subsidized" loans for parents, but there are subsidized loans for students. There's more on this subject later, but the bottom line is that with a subsidized loan, the federal government will pay the interest while the student's in school.

Parents' Loans

Now that you have some background, we're going to talk about parents' loans first. They're easier to discuss because there is less variety. Parents' loans are called "Plus" loans (that stands for "parent's loans for undergraduate students"). Parents qualify for these loans under the following circumstances:

❑ They have a child who is a dependent undergraduate student and who is attending college at least half time.

❑ They have an adequate credit history allowing them to qualify for the loan, or are able to find a friend or relative who does and is willing to co-sign on their loan.

❑ Both the student and the parents meet general aid eligibility requirements, such as being U.S. citizens who are not in default on another government debt.

Loan Limits

The maximum amount parents can borrow in any given year equals the total cost of attending school, minus other financial aid received by the student. In other words, if the total cost of college was $10,000, including tuition, fees, books, and so on, and the student received $5,000 in aid, the parents could borrow $5,000 through the Plus program.

Interest Rates and Fees

The interest rate on Plus loans issued after 1998 is variable. It's reset once annually in July based on market interest rates on ninety-day Treasury bills in the final auction in May. In the summer of 2002, that brought loan rates to their lowest levels in history. The interest rate on Plus loans taken out after July 1, 1998, fell to 4.86 percent. (That rate was available from July 2002 through June 30, 2003.)

Loans secured before mid-1998 were governed by a slightly different set of rules. As a result, the rate on older Plus loans is usually about one-half percentage point higher.

When rates change, lenders notify borrowers of the new rate and the effective date. As with most loans, interest is charged from the date of the first disbursement until the loan is paid off.

Fees of up to 4 percent of the loan amount can be charged on parents' loans. This fee (part of which goes to the federal government and part to the guaranty agency responsible for repaying the loan in the event of a default) is deducted directly from loan disbursements.

Payment of Loan Proceeds

The loan money generally is sent directly to the school, not the parent. The loan proceeds are first applied against any outstanding debt the student has from tuition, fees, room, board, or other school charges. If there is money left over, the school will send a check to the parents, unless the parents have authorized the school to put the money in the student's school account.

Repayment

Parents are generally required to begin repaying their loans within sixty days of the final loan disbursement. They usually are given four payment choices—a standard, extended, or graduated repayment plan and an income-sensitive option.

❑ **Standard repayment** is based on paying a set amount each month, which will never be less than $50. This plan aims to pay off the loan in ten years or less.

❑ **Extended repayment,** available only to those with substantial debt, allows borrowers to stretch their payments over as long as twenty-five years. You have to owe more than $30,000 on loans taken out after October 7, 1998, to qualify.

❑ **Graduated repayment** sets initial payments low, at roughly the cost of the interest that's accruing; the payments then gradually rise. The benefit to this plan: If you have a child in the early years of school, it keeps payments low while your expenses are the highest because you're trying to swing tuition along with everything else. It allows the payments to rise later, presumably after the child has graduated and you're better able to afford them.

❑ **Income-sensitive repayment** is slightly less simple to quantify. Parents who feel they can't make the payment schedules under the other repayment options must get a form from their lender. The lender will have them report their income and expenses to determine how much they'll have to pay on the student debt. The monthly debt payments must amount to at least the interest accruing on the account. However, there are few other standards. Also, these plans are usually periodically reviewed by the lender, with an eye to boosting the monthly payments to meet what would be required under the more typical formulas.

Deferment, Forbearance, and Cancellation

Parents who experience a serious economic hardship can request loan deferment or forbearance, just like student borrowers. Deferment puts your payments on hold for a set period of time. Forbearance can reduce or postpone payments as well. Neither process is automatic. You must apply for a deferment or forbearance with your lender or with the Department of Education, depending upon who made the loan.

Generally speaking, deferments will be granted if the student for whom the money was borrowed returns to school at least half time, is in a graduate or fellowship program, is unemployed, or finds that he cannot meet his loan payments because of severe economic hardship. The standards for forbearance are a little looser. They can also include poor health and unforeseen personal problems.

Plus loans can be cancelled if the borrower is permanently and totally disabled or if the student for whom the money was borrowed dies. In some rare circumstances, the loan could also be cancelled, if the school closes before the student is able to complete her course of study.

Bankruptcy generally *does not* wipe out student debt. Student debts can be eliminated through bankruptcy only if the judge determines that continued repayment would cause undue hardship on the borrower.

Loans for Students

There are two main types of federal loans for undergraduate students: Federal Perkins Loans and Stafford Loans. Perkins Loans are provided only to needy students. They offer a set interest rate for the life of the loan. Stafford Loans can be obtained by virtually anyone, needy or not, because they come in two varieties: subsidized and unsubsidized.

Both subsidized and unsubsidized Stafford Loans bear variable interest rates, which are adjusted once annually. The main difference between the two: During periods of deferment, the federal government pays the interest on subsidized Stafford Loans. With unsubsidized Stafford Loans, the interest builds up for the student to pay later.

Perkins Loans

A Perkins Loan would be included in your financial aid package if you are a needy student who qualifies. This loan offers a low 5 percent fixed interest rate and is made by the school with both federal and school funds.

Your total borrowing limit under the Perkins Loan program varies based on your need and the school's funding. However, the maximum amount any individual student can borrow under the Perkins Loan program is $4,000 per year, and no more than $20,000 during the entire course of undergraduate study. Graduate students can borrow up to $6,000 per year, to a maximum of $40,000. That $40,000 limit includes any Perkins Loans from undergraduate years.

There are no administrative fees for taking out the loan, although if your payments are late, you could be charged a late fee. Payments are not required on these loans until nine months after you leave school, graduate, or drop below half-time status. Perkins Loans are generally paid back over a ten-year period. But like other student loans, they can be deferred, put into forbearance, or consolidated. Consolidation would change the terms of the loan. For information on how these terms change, see the section in this chapter titled "Consolidating Your Loans" on page 212.

Stafford Loans

Like the Plus loan program, Stafford Loans are offered both directly through the Department of Education and through outside lenders in the FFEL program. Loan rates are variable, ranging from about 4 percent today to the maximum rate of 8.25 percent.

The first step to qualify for a Stafford Loan is to fill out the FAFSA form. The data you put on that form largely determines whether you get subsidized or unsubsidized Staffords.

Loan limits. Loan limits depend on the year of study and the year of application. For instance, in the 2001–2002 academic year, the maximum Stafford Loan amount for a college freshman was $2,625. Sophomores could receive up to $3,500, and juniors and seniors could borrow up to $5,500.

The loan limits are higher if you are an independent student—parents are gone or no longer willing or able to provide for the sudent's support—or if your parents don't qualify for Plus loans. Independent freshmen can get up to $6,625 and sophomores up to $7,500, while juniors and seniors can borrow a maximum of $10,500 per year. Graduate students can borrow up to $18,500 per year under the Stafford program.

The loans also are subject to lifetime caps. Dependent undergraduate students can borrow a maximum of $23,000 under the Stafford program over the course of their entire college career. Independent undergrads can borrow up to a maximum of $46,000, while graduate and professional students can borrow up to $138,500.

Loan limits are subject to change, as are all the terms of all student-aid programs. But the changes must be approved by Congress and usually are made only when Department of Education funding is revisited, roughly once every five years.

Interest rates and fees. Just like parents' loans, interest rates on Stafford Loans are set annually based on Treasury rates in late May. New rate information comes out on July 1 and is good until June 30 of the following year.

A fee of up to 4 percent of the loan amount is taken from each disbursement. That fee pays the federal government and the guaranty association that backs your loan. If you don't make loan payments on time, you could also be subject to late payment and collection fees.

Repayment. Repayments must begin on Stafford Loans six months after you leave school, graduate, or drop below half-time status. If you go back to school in the meantime or are unable to find work, you can put your loans into deferment. This simply halts collection of principal and interest payments until you graduate again or get a job.

There are four repayment options for both FFELP borrowers and those who borrow through the direct loan program. Three of them are identical. The final one—income-contingent or income-sensitive repayment—is slightly different, depending on the loan program:

❏ **Standard repayment** requires that you pay a set monthly amount, which is never less than $50 per month. The program is aimed at paying off the debt completely within ten years.

❏ **Extended repayment,** which is available to those with substantial loans, allows you to stretch repayment over twenty-five years.

❏ **Graduated repayment** allows you to start off with small payments—as little as the interest accruing on the loan—and build to bigger payments, presumably when you've got a higher-paying job and are better able to pay.

❏ **Income-contingent repayment** plans base your repayment amount on your income, family size, and loan amount. Your loan payments will rise with your income, but if you are unable to completely pay off the loans within twenty-five years, any remaining balance will be forgiven. This repayment option is offered only through the direct loan program.

❑ **Income-sensitive repayment** is similar to the income-contingent repayment plan, but there's no formula for forgiving the debt after a set period. These plans are also generally reviewed once annually (or on some other regular schedule) to see if the borrower's income has risen enough to qualify for one of the more typical options.

Repayment incentives. Some lenders will reduce the interest rate on Stafford loans if the student agrees to automatic debits—payments coming directly out of a checking or savings account—or if the student maintains a perfect payment record over the first several years of repayment. Most lenders provide information about these incentives with packets of loan information provided to borrowers a few months before their loan grace periods end. However, if your lender does not provide information about incentives, ask. It never hurts and can potentially save you several hundred dollars over the life of the loan.

Loan Forgiveness

There are several programs that will forgive all—or a portion—of a student's debts if the student goes into particular professions or volunteers her time. Lenders have information about loan-forgiveness programs, although they may not provide this information automatically. If you think you qualify, ask.

Here's a rundown of the programs that affect a large number of former students:

Child Care Workers

Child care workers who complete at least two consecutive years of full-time employment in a school serving a predominantly low-income community can have up to 100 percent of their Stafford

Loan obligations forgiven or paid by the Department of Education. To qualify, the child care worker must:

❑ Have been a new borrower as of October 1, 1998, which means he could not have an outstanding balance under the Stafford Loan program at that point.
❑ Have obtained a bachelor's degree in early childhood education.
❑ Have worked for at least two consecutive years as a child care provider serving a low-income community prior to applying for loan forgiveness.
❑ May not have received similar benefits under the Americorps program, a program that offers scholarships or money with which to pay back student loans in return for a year of community service.

If all of these qualification standards are met, the child care worker can apply to have a portion of his Stafford Loan balances forgiven each year. The program pays off the loans in increments: 20 percent after two years of qualifying employment, another 20 percent after three years, 30 percent more after four years, and the final 30 percent after completing five years of eligible work.

This program is offered on a first-come, first-served basis and is contingent on receiving sufficient federal funding. Those who receive forgiveness in one year are given priority for loan-forgiveness dollars in subsequent years.

Teachers

Elementary and secondary school teachers who work in low-income communities for at least five years can be eligible for up to $5,000 in loan forgiveness on their *Stafford* debts. To qualify, the teacher must:

❑ Have been a new borrower as of October 1, 1998.
❑ Have been a full-time teacher for five years in a school serving a low-income area, as listed in the *Annual Directory of Designated Low-Income Schools.*

❑ Be teaching a subject relevant to his academic major, if a secondary school teacher.

❑ Have demonstrated knowledge and teaching skills in basic areas of elementary curriculum, such as reading, writing, and arithmetic, if an elementary school teacher.

Up to 100 percent of *Perkins Loan* debts can be cancelled for teachers who:

❑ Serve in a full-time capacity in a school geared for students from low-income families.

❑ Teach special education.

❑ Or teach a subject area for which there is a shortage of qualified teachers, such as mathematics, foreign language, or bilingual education.

Vista and Peace Corps Volunteers

Up to 70 percent of your loans can be cancelled if you serve in the Peace Corps or Vista—a domestic volunteer program similar to the Peace Corps. Like the loan-forgiveness program for child care workers, this program erases debt in increments. Fifteen percent of the original principal amount, plus interest, is wiped away for those who serve a full year; another 15 percent is wiped away after the second year; 20 percent more after the third year; and a final 20 percent will be forgiven for those who complete four years of service.

Armed Forces

Members of the military can qualify for up to 50 percent loan forgiveness if they are active-duty personnel in areas of hostilities or imminent danger. The cancellation rate works out to 12.5 percent of the loan amount per full year of service.

Other Programs

Peace officers, health care workers, and people who provide early-intervention services for the disabled can also qualify for loan-discharge programs, given the right circumstances. If you are working in any of these fields, contact your lender or the Department of Education for more information.

Consolidating Your Loans

Once out of school, students are likely to get bombarded with information about loan consolidation. Consolidation programs allow the borrower to simplify repayment by combining a variety of different types of student loans into one. Consolidation has a couple of other benefits, too. For example, you can lower your required monthly payments by stretching repayment out over longer periods. The more debt you have, the more time you get to repay.

The second significant advantage is that consolidation makes your loans fixed rate. The interest rate on the consolidation loan will be the weighted average rate on all the consolidated loans, *rounded up* to the next eighth of a percentage point. By law, this rate can never exceed 8.25 percent.

As mentioned before, the interest rate on unconsolidated Stafford and Plus loans is variable, changing once annually based on market interest rates. If market interest rates rise, so, too, will the cost of your student loans. The rate on consolidation loans is fixed at the time of consolidation at the weighted average rate on all of the consolidated loans.

If you graduate during a low-interest rate period, it may make sense to consolidate your loans simply to lock in that low rate. But beware: Once you lock in an interest rate through loan consolidation, you cannot refinance these student loans again to get an even lower rate. If interest rates fall further, you're out of luck. Once secured, your consolidation loan rate will never change.

Who Can Consolidate

Generally, student loans can be consolidated only after the borrower has graduated. The one exception is with the direct loan program, which allows consolidation even while the student remains in school, as long as the student is attending school at least half-time and has at least one FFELP or direct loan to consolidate.

Oddly enough, you don't need multiple loans to consolidate. If you have just one student loan that you want to convert from a variable-rate debt to a fixed-rate debt, you can "consolidate" it into a new fixed-rate loan. There are no fees, aside from the rounded-up interest rate, so there's very little downside, other than the fact that you can't cut your interest rate by consolidating this same loan again.

How to Consolidate

Loan consolidation programs are offered by a wide variety of lenders, who are likely to compete for your business. However, generally you must consolidate with one of your existing lenders. The exception: You can consolidate with the direct loan program, if none of your existing lenders offer an income-contingent repayment plan that you can work with.

Otherwise, you're free to pick and choose among your existing stable of lenders for the one you'd like to continue doing business with. Look for a lender that's responsive to your questions, appears to provide accurate and helpful service, and provides attractive options for you, such as automatic payments and Web-based account management.

Credit Cards

They're not student loans, per se, but it would be remiss in today's day and age to talk about student loans without making at least a passing reference to credit cards. Over the past several years, college campuses have become massive recruiting grounds for credit card customers. Students get credit applications in their book bags and dormitory mailboxes. Fraternities sponsor credit card sign-ups as house fund-raisers. Students are offered everything from coffee mugs to sweatshirts to accept this "free" credit.

Beware. Interest rates on student credit cards are some of the highest in the nation, running from 19.9 percent to more than 25 percent. If you go over your credit limit, you're likely to suffer a $15 to $30 fee, although your credit card company may be perfectly happy to raise your credit limit into the thousands of dollars, regardless of whether or not you have a job. Pay late and you get hit with another $30 fee.

Minimum payments are often set low, at about 2 percent of the outstanding balance. That does two things: It keeps payments deceptively low and allows the borrower to stay in debt for decades, paying for yesterday's pleasures many times over in interest and fees.

Why would lenders give you so much credit before you even have a steady job? Again, there are two reasons: First, responsible people tend to be loyal to the first company that issued them credit. Second, issuers believe that you or your parents will make every effort to pay your credit card debts, because if you don't, the bad credit rating that you'd get for not paying can dog you during a very pivotal period of your life.

"Charge-It" Consequences

If you make payments late, or default on credit card debts, the late and missing payments will be noted on your credit report. Your credit report is a document used by lenders, insurers, employers, landlords, and others. These people and companies report how you've handled credit with them and seek information on how you've handled credit with others.

Generally speaking, the data on your credit report gets fed into a computer program to determine your so-called FICO score. This FICO score is a rating ranging from 300 to 900, which aims to handicap your propensity to pay your bills. If you have a low score—anything under about 600—you'll pay more for auto loans, mortgages, and auto insurance. A bad credit rating can also hamper your ability to rent an apartment or get a job. Prospective employers are able to look at your credit report, as are landlords, credit grantors, and insurers.

What leads to a low score? In a student's case, the first issue is youth. The less credit history you have, the lower your score. Nevertheless, you can overcome a so-called "thin file" by simply paying whatever bills you accumulate promptly and reliably. Make a few payments late, however, and your score will plunge. The cost of future loans will soar, and employers may look at you suspiciously and choose other applicants with better credit histories over you when given a choice between two equally qualified applicants.

The moral of this story: If you obtain a credit card on campus, use it sparingly. Pay it off monthly. Tell your parents, immediately, if you find yourself in credit trouble. Yes, they'll probably get angry. But the alternatives are worse. Be smart enough to recognize credit problems before they get out of control and before they affect the next decade of your life.

chapter 13

Private Scholarships

CHRIS VUTURO HAS NEWS FOR THE MILLIONS OF AMERicans who believe that college scholarships go only to the needy, the academically gifted, or to talented athletes. There's big money to be had by middle-class students who are simply willing to work at it, he says.

He should know. By the time Vuturo was a twenty-eight-year-old graduate student, he had won some $885,000 in college scholarships during an admittedly lengthy college career. That allowed him to graduate from Harvard with just $6,000 in debt, despite Harvard's $100,000 four-year price tag, and despite the fact that neither he nor his family had money saved for school.

"It comes down to a question of effort," he says. "If you put out the effort, good things are going to happen."

Tavia Evans has a similar story. By the time she was a twenty-one-year-old journalism student at Northwestern University in Evanston, Illinois, she had received $100,000 in college scholarships and grants.

Both Vuturo and Evans are unusual people. Committed, qualified, and highly ambitious, they pursued scholarships with vigor. But they both learned a lesson that every college student should know: There is a wealth of private money aimed at helping students finance school. The myth is that the money goes unclaimed. In fact, there are usually dozens—sometimes hundreds of thousands—of applicants for *each* award.

This money comes from a vast array of sources—companies, trade groups, fraternities, sororities, credit unions, clubs, wealthy individuals, and foundations, to name just a few. In some cases, it's distributed based on need. However, often the scholarships go to a student who happens to have a personal interest or connection that the group wants to foster. Here are some examples:

❑ The American Society of Women Accountants gives $1,500 to $2,500 scholarships each year to college sophomores, juniors, or seniors who have declared accounting as their major and have spent at least sixty hours studying it.

❑ The Automotive Hall of Fame grants between twenty and twenty-five scholarships annually, ranging from $250 to $2,000, to college students interested in an automotive career.

❑ Microsoft provides a scholarship covering 100 percent of the cost of tuition for a year for a student who completes a salaried summer internship at the company's Redmond, Washington, headquarters.

❑ The Aviation Distributors and Manufacturers Association provides $1,000 a year to two students who are studying aviation management or to be a pilot.

There are scholarships for those who study wine making and for those who study history and attend school in East Texas. Also, there's a highly lucrative award for Florida residents studying nursing. Another scholarship is good for any course of study, if you study in Florida and happen to be either Nicaraguan or Haitian. Children of members of the Rotary Club or the Knights of Columbus could be eligible for scholarship money. So could kids who like to invent gadgets that use a battery or who drink Coca-Cola.

Finding Your Niche

The trick to finding private scholarships and grants is figuring out how you fit within the bigger world. To whom and which organizations are you connected? Are you affiliated with a church, synagogue, mosque, or other religious organization? A member of a particular ethnic group? Have you chosen a major? Have you done volunteer work? Joined clubs? Are your parents involved in clubs, trade groups, or other organizations? Where do they bank? Where do your parents work? Teachers, peace officers, and firemen have funded dozens of scholarships for children of other teachers, peace officers, and firemen. And many other employers and employee groups provide scholarships, too.

Are you an academic star? An athlete? Are you willing to dedicate time during school or after graduation to do volunteer work? Are you willing to join the military? Do you have a job?

All of these factors will have a big impact on whether or not you can find a private scholarship to help defray your costs. It's worth noting that many of the scholarships are relatively small—$100, $500, or $1,000, for example. But they're well worth trying for, says Evans. "Apply for a lot of the ones that say they are only for $500 or $1,000, because you need all (the money) you can get in college," she says. "You should apply for a dollar."

Risks and Rewards of Private Awards

There are two big benefits to private scholarships: They don't need to be paid back, and most of them are portable. Only a relative handful of the thousands of private scholarships offered are linked to a particular school or university, although some do require residency in a particular state or geographic area.

They do, however, count as aid. A student who receives a private

219

scholarship or award should inform the financial-aid counselor at her school. This scholarship reduces the other aid that this student gets. However, because private scholarships can replace loans and work study, that's well worth doing. After all, a grant is better than a loan.

Getting Started

To help with your search, prepare a worksheet that lists three people: Student, Mom, and Dad. Run through all the pertinent facts for each of you, including your ethnic background, religious affiliations, and organizations that you're involved with through either work or play. The forms on the following pages can help you get started.

Finding a Private Award

Vuturo and Evans took different routes to find their scholarships. He spent hours in the public library. She spent hours on the Web. Either method can provide a great result.

Those who choose the library approach should look for two books:

❑ *The Scholarship Advisor* by Chris Vuturo, (Princeton Review) was in its fifth edition at press time. It's updated annually and lists thousands of scholarships and awards. The sheer volume of information makes Vuturo's book a bit tough to navigate when looking for a particular type of award. However, it's notable because Vuturo also provides advice, drawn from his own voluminous experience, on applying for awards, writing scholarship essays, and what scholarship committees are seeking. The explanatory text is clear, practical, and invaluable for students who need guidance in how to approach the topic.

❑ The College Board's *Scholarship Handbook* also provides annually updated information about literally thousands of private

WORKSHEET

Background Data on Student

Age:_____*

College status (year and full or part time): _____

Employer: _____

Ethnic background: _____

Religious affiliation: _____

Clubs: _____

_____

_____

_____

Volunteer activities:_____

_____

_____

_____

_____

_____

Sorority/fraternity affiliation:_____

Prospective major: _____

Sports:_____

_____

Hobbies/other interests: _____

Special circumstances (disabled/orphaned/blind) _____

_____

_____

*Some scholarships are dedicated to older students who return to study after spending some time in the working world or raising kids. If you're a returning student, keep an eye out.

WORKSHEET

Background Data on Mom

Employer: _____

Former Employer: _____

Religious affiliation: _____

Professional affiliations and memberships: _____
_____
_____

Clubs/interests: _____
_____
_____

Volunteer activities: _____
_____
_____
_____
_____
_____

Sorority affiliation: _____

awards. The book is nicely organized, allowing students to find scholarships and internships quickly that dovetail with their field of study, ethnic background, and interests. Notably, the College Board also shows how many awards have been given and how many applied for those awards, when that information is available. It's a nice snapshot of your odds.

❑ Evans also suggests that students simply look for directories listing private foundations. They are generally named after a donor such as John Ross Foundation, Isplat Inland Foundation, Jackson Foundation, or my favorite—Kosciuszko Foundation. Foundations often sponsor scholarships for needy students. If you have trouble finding what you need, ask a reference librarian to help.

WORKSHEET

Background Data on Dad

Employer: _____

Former Employer: _____

Religious affiliation: _____

Professional affiliations and memberships: _____
_____
_____

Clubs/interests: _____
_____
_____

Volunteer activities: _____
_____
_____
_____
_____
_____

Fraternity affiliation: _____

Web Searches

Evans searched for scholarships on the Web through a site called FastWeb (www.fastweb.com). FastWeb functions off a long questionnaire that aims to match students with scholarships offered by companies, clubs, fraternities, trade groups, and other organizations offering private awards. The benefit of this search is that it's relatively painless. It takes about a half hour to complete the application. Then it's just two more clicks, and you've got the results of your search.

Depending on the student's interests and activities, as well as the clubs, companies, and trade groups that her parents are involved with, this search could come back with anywhere from one to fifty potential matches. The student, however, must weed through the matches to make sure that she actually qualifies. Some matches don't match—they've simply come up as a match because the student delivered a glancing blow at some portion of the qualification standards. For instance, plug into the website that you're Catholic and have Czechoslovakian roots, and you're likely to learn about the First Catholic Slovak Ladies Association award. But alas—it requires potential applicants to be members to get a scholarship. If you're not an FCSLA member, there's no money for you. Don't be discouraged, though. There will probably be plenty of valid matches, too.

The down side to a FastWeb search is that the site is supported by advertising. At nearly every break between screens, you're asked if you'd like to receive somebody's promotional materials. Unless you click No, Thank You, you'll end up on endless Internet mailing lists.

The College Board offers another good website for scholarship searches. Go to www.collegeboard.com and click on Paying for College. A second prompt leads to the organization's Scholarship Search. Like FastWeb's search engine, you'll get some matches that don't work for you. Nevertheless, there will be plenty of scholarships that do, and many that you've most likely never heard of before. And, with a few more clicks, the site tells you where to apply, how much you could get, and all about the qualification standards. Like virtually everything sponsored by the College Board, the service is first-class.

Applying for Awards

Students who have won private scholarships and awards generally point to personal contacts, letters of recommendation, and essays as being key determinants. When the grant is not based on need, scholarship committees often ask applicants for an essay, Vuturo says.

The All-Important Essay

What the scholarship committees are looking for in that essay is not a reiteration of your qualifications, but a glimpse of your character, Vuturo adds. Those who can clearly define what makes them unique and somehow more worthy than the hundreds of other applicants seeking aid are far more likely to win scholarships.

Consider the seminal moments in your life, he suggests. What are the things that changed you and made you a better person? Think of experiences that you believe helped you grow. Going waterskiing with your parents, while fun, probably is not the type of experience that matters. But if you have volunteered at a convalescent home, or helped tutor children or teach them to read, these could be great experiences to draw on for these essays.

Never exaggerate or lie in your essay or during an interview with the scholarship committee, Vuturo cautions. Be honest and earnest, well-groomed, and polite. First impressions matter.

Connections

Evans also suggests that you develop a source in your school's financial-aid office that you can go to whenever you need help. In her case, an African-American aid counselor took Evans under her wing and went to bat for her whenever it mattered. Evans believes this helped her get scholarships she wasn't even aware of—some of which were offered through the school but were not advertised—and helped her get a chance to study abroad.

She also made a point of asking about scholarships at the bank, the credit union, the Rotary Club—any and every local organization and business that might offer one. That's important, she says, because people at these companies and organizations actually know you. They are likely to go the distance for you and may choose your application over another qualified applicant simply because of that personal contact. You don't have that edge when applying for national scholarships and grants. In addition, although the national awards often offer more money, they're also highly competitive, Evans notes pragmatically. In some cases, thousands of students will compete for just a dozen awards. The local awards are more likely to be for $250 or $500, but there may be only a dozen applicants. Your odds of getting several of these are fairly good.

Scholarship Scams

Over the past half dozen years, a host of companies have sprung up promising "guaranteed" scholarships. All you have to do is send them an enrollment fee, and they say they'll provide you with scads of scholarship dollars.

Don't be deceived. According to the Federal Trade Commission, which launched a crackdown on these operations a few years ago, *any service that promises you scholarship money in exchange for an up-front fee is nothing but a scam.*

In many cases, these so-called scholarship search services did nothing more for the $250 to $300 they charged than provide the student with the scholarship information that he could have received for free on the Web or in the library. In some cases, they simply took the fee and disappeared.

Simple advice: Don't pay for a scholarship search. It's money wasted, money that could have been used for college. Also realize that no one can apply for scholarships on your behalf. Students must do this themselves.

Apply Early and Often

One last bit of advice: Get started as early as possible. The competition to receive private grants and aid is stiff and gets stiffer every year, says Evans. Ideally, you want to start thinking about and investigating the possibilities a full year before you enroll in college. In fact, many private scholarships have January 1 deadlines—that's

January 1 of the year *before* school starts. The longer you wait, the fewer options you have.

There are plenty of options, though. Make sure you apply for any scholarship that you can possibly qualify for. Students shouldn't knock themselves out of the running for any scholarship just because they think it's a long shot.

"The saddest thing is when people think they can't get any scholarships, so they don't even try," Vuturo says. "At least try. Even if you don't get the scholarship, it prepares you for the college application process, and it prepares you for applying for more scholarships later."

PART FOUR

Other Alternatives and Key Resources

chapter 14

Making Lemonade

S O YOU'VE READ THIS WHOLE BOOK AND CONCLUDED THAT you started too late. You can't possibly save enough for college. The research you've done so far tells you that aid won't come close to covering your costs, and you don't have relatives rich enough to finance a trust fund on your or your child's behalf. Now what?

College is still possible—without going into lifelong debt—for those who are willing to work at it and make some compromises. Here's a laundry list of things to do.

Consider Community College

John Bushman, a retired father of three, said community colleges allowed his brood to effectively cut the cost of postsecondary education in half. His two oldest children completed their general education requirements at a nearby community college; his youngest plans to do the same. Bushman estimated that the choice saved him

$10,000 per year, per child. In his case, that works out to a tidy $60,000.

The choice is not only economical, it's common, says Terry Hartle, senior vice president of the American Council on Education in Washington, D.C. At any given point in time, roughly 40 percent of the nation's college students are attending community colleges.

Some stop there because they're able to earn two-year degrees that suit their career requirements. Some are also adults, attending for fun or continuing education. Others are budget-conscious high school graduates who intend to go on to four-year universities, like Bushman's offspring. These students save themselves and their families a fortune and often benefit in other ways, too.

The Cost

The average cost of tuition and fees in the 2002–2003 academic year was $1,735 per year at a two-year public college, according to the College Board. That's roughly half the cost of tuition and fees at a four-year public university and a fraction of the tuition expense at four-year private colleges, which charged an average of $18,273 annually, according to College Board data.

However, it's not just the tuition and fees that provide the savings. Because community colleges are ubiquitous and local, students have the option of commuting to class from home. That saves the cost of renting and furnishing an apartment. The academic standards of community colleges are comparable to the standards set at four-year universities. Like four-year schools, there are excellent, fair, and poor two-year colleges. There are some that are exceptional in particular fields of study and marginal in others. However, general education units taken at accredited two-year colleges usually are transferable to four-year universities.

Students planning to transfer should talk to a guidance counselor before signing up for classes, however. Not all schools accept all transfer units for all majors all the time. If you or your child aim to graduate from a particular four-year school, the guidance

232

counselor can help structure a course load that will transfer.

There's another benefit to attending community college: It may help the student qualify for admittance at a college or university that would have rejected her application when she was in high school, experts maintain. Why?

Colleges get graded, just as the students who attend them do. The criteria for college rankings are based partly on graduation rates, says Jack Joyce, director of guidance services at the College Board. A student who has successfully completed two years at a community college is far more likely to graduate after transferring to a four-year school than a student who starts a four-year program straight out of high school, he points out.

As a result, many colleges that rejected a high school senior will throw their doors open to that same student after he has completed two years at a community college with decent grades. In fact, top-notch state universities are increasingly forging alliances with community colleges by promising the colleges' graduates priority admission, he says.

Take Advanced Placement Classes

Juniors and seniors in high school can save themselves (or their parents) up to a year's worth of college costs and time if they take advanced placement classes in high school. Advanced placement classes are demanding academic courses offered at most good high schools. The courses, which stress fundamentals such as mathematics, language, science, and history, provide both high school and college credit.

The catch: To get the college credit, the student must take (or obtain a particular numerical rank on) an AP exam at the end of the course. And, although most colleges accept AP classes for college credit based on exam scores, a few do not, or they restrict the number of units granted for the class to something less than what would be earned if the student took the same course in college.

There is a fee to take the examination. However, those with economic need may be able to have the fees waived. Students can get details on which AP classes are offered, and whether aid is available for the examination fees, from their high school guidance counselor.

In a best-case scenario, an ambitious student could shave a semester, or even a year, from her college requirements by consistently taking AP classes and passing the tests. Because you're paying fees to take AP tests, and you're shaving—at best—one year off the four-year college bill, AP classes don't cut the tuition costs as much as going to junior college. However, if you're determined to spend your college years at the four-year institution of your choice, you may graduate earlier with this route, which puts you on track to get a job a year earlier, too.

What if you don't pass the AP tests (or make the grade in terms of numerical score)? If you received a decent grade in the class, it's still likely to help you. Many colleges give more weight to the grades a student received in an AP class than an ordinary class, because the classes tend to be more challenging. Consequently, a "B" in an AP class may be worth almost as much as an "A" in an ordinary high school class. The bottom line: Successfully completing AP courses in high school can get you into a better college.

Consider Distance Learning

Bjarne Jensen earned a bachelor's degree in finance for less than $5,000—a bargain price for a four-year education. His secret: distance learning. He took a series of correspondence courses and course exams. The combination cost him about $12 a unit.

Distance learning is becoming an increasingly viable option for Web-savvy students who either can't or don't want to participate in the campus experience, says Jeanne Jensen, who now helps operate a website at www.colleges-without-classes.com. Roughly 1,500 degrees can be had at 176 accredited colleges, she adds. Some of those colleges charge regular tuition and fees for attending online classes, but the student saves room, board, and transportation costs.

Jensen also economized on his book expenses by checking textbooks out of public libraries. In systematic fashion, he found out which books would be required, requesting them through interlibrary loans when they weren't readily available. Because interlibrary loans are available only in two-week stretches, he'd make sequential requests for the same book when he thought he'd need it for more than two weeks.

The benefit of this type of program for learners like Bjarne Jensen is clear: You can study when it's convenient, thus holding down your day job or caring for your children while earning a college degree. For younger students, it may not be the best answer because you miss the fun of being on campus. However, some schools and classes do offer get-togethers and in-person study groups. Certainly, for someone on a tight schedule or a tight budget, it may be worth considering.

Those who want to know more about distance learning can find out whether their favorite school offers Internet-based options, or they can search the Web for colleges with classes in cyberspace. Jeanne Jensen's website can also do a search for you, by matching your course of study to the colleges registered in the program. The one catch: The system will match your interests to degree programs for free, but to find out which colleges offer those degrees, there's a $5 fee. That fee allows the site to operate without advertising, Jensen says.

Budget

None of those sound like viable options? Here's a thought. If you want to reduce the cost of college and cut your required family contribution to college bills, you can simply spend less.

Sounds weird, but here's how it works. Financial aid for college students is based on the all-in cost of college. That's room, board,

235

tuition, fees, books, transportation, and incidentals. Colleges estimate the fungible costs—everything but tuition and fees—to help aid officials tabulate each family's need. They're usually pretty generous in their estimates.

If you can find a way to spend less than the college estimates, you cut costs from your and your family's expected contribution. In other words, if you attend the University of California at Santa Barbara, where the estimated cost for books is $1,210, but you buy books used or borrow them from the library and manage to spend just $600, the $610 you save comes from your own pocket. It does not reduce your financial aid. You simply don't have to pay it.

The same holds true for the estimated costs with room and board, which commonly run from $6,000 to $8,000. If you share a cheap apartment and buy your groceries with coupons, you might easily shave $1,000 or even $2,000 off the estimated tab for room and board. While financial aid has to look at the estimates, you don't have to live by them. The more you put yourself on a budget, the less you pay, the less you have to borrow, and the better off you are in the long run. It's a good lesson for life.

Pay Monthly

If the issue isn't the cost—rather, it's coming up with the cost in one lump sum at the beginning of the school year—you should realize that most schools offer some sort of monthly payment plan. Many schools contract with outside companies, such as Academic Management Systems, to provide the billing services. At those schools, you'd pay a one-time enrollment fee, usually $50. After that, your tuition bill simply will be divided into ten or twelve equal monthly payments. No interest is charged for this service.

Alternately, some schools provide monthly payment plans on their own, usually saving the parent the service fee. If paying monthly would alleviate some of your college-cost stress, call your school and inquire.

A few schools suggest that you pay the bill with a credit card because they don't offer a monthly payment plan. Don't do it. The interest rate on your credit card is certain to be far higher than the interest charged on any type of student loan. If you need to borrow, borrow through student loans.

Get a Job

Sure, you can use a work-study program. Thanks to the award on your financial-aid application, they're offering you a minimum wage job in the campus library, where you can study when you're not stamping expiration dates on books or snarling at campus rowdies. But if you're an ambitious student on a budget, you might be better off looking for higher-paid work elsewhere.

The downside of working off-campus is that you'll have to make your school schedule accommodate your work schedule. For most employers, that means you'll need fairly predictable hours. Creating a course load that allows you to finish your classroom time at noon—or just attend classes two or three days a week—can be a scheduling challenge. But it's possible. Meanwhile, off-campus jobs provide two big benefits: wages that usually exceed minimum wage and work experience that you can use to get future employment.

Many a family has financed college by putting the parent who had been home with the toddlers and teens back into the paying work world. If you or your parent is contemplating going back to work to finance college, it would be wise to consider whether there are any viable opportunities at the college that you hope to attend. Many private colleges provide steep discounts or even free tuition to the offspring of their employees. These programs may have minimum service requirements—for example, the employee must have been with the college for a year or more to qualify. However, if they are available, the free or discounted tuition can be an extremely valuable perk. In any event, it's an option worth checking into.

Volunteer

If you are service oriented, committing yourself to spending a year or more serving your community or a big national charity can pay off in both personal satisfaction and cash. The AmeriCorps program, for example, provides thousands of individuals either with education scholarships or with awards to pay back student loans every year. The program usually provides health insurance, a modest living allowance, and $4,725 to help pay for college or pay back student loans. Some 50,000 individuals join the program every year, serving in areas ranging from low-income housing to spousal abuse. To get more information about what's available and how to sign up, point your Web browser to www.americorps.org. AmeriCorps works with a variety of national, state, and local organizations with operations in virtually every major city in the country.

Join the Army

OK, not everyone is willing to risk getting shot at to pay for college. But if you're adventurous, brave, capable, and able to take orders, it may make sense to look into ROTC programs or enlistment.

If you are a promising candidate, you could have four years at a prestigious college, such as West Point, fully paid. You'll serve four years in the armed services after graduation, but if you think that's a possibility anyway, it's worth looking into the admissions prospects in advance. The military often provides specialized technical training and military service looks great on the resumé, too. Most schools have an ROTC office or a campus recruiter who can provide more information or answer questions.

chapter 15

Resources

529 Plans

There are two master websites that provide detailed information on how 529 plans work and provide links and information about the various state plans:

❑ **www.savingforcollege.com,** operated by accountant Joseph Hurley, who has written a book on 529 plans (*The Best Way to Save for College: A Complete Guide to 529 Plans,* BonaCom Publications, 2002; $26.95) and has opened no fewer than twenty-one accounts for his own children. In addition to the plethora of well-organized information, this site is recommended for its "hat ratings" of the various state 529 plans. One rating ranks the plan for in-state residents; a second rating ranks how well out-of-state residents fare with the program. These are invaluable tools for those who want to winnow 529 choices to a manageable few before requesting more details from the plans themselves.

❑ **www.collegesavings.org,** operated by the College Savings Plan Network, an association of state treasurers dedicated to helping people explore 529 options. The site isn't as user-friendly as Hurley's, but some of the information is more up-to-date.

Facts and Contact Information for Individual State Plans*

* As of January 2003. Some plans may raise investment limits annually.

Alabama
Maximum investment: $269,000 per beneficiary
Minimum investment: $25 per month
Contact: Online at www.treasury.state.al.us or by phone at
334-242-7500 or 866-529-2228

Alaska
Maximum investment: $250,000 per beneficiary
Minimum investment: $50 per month
Contact: Online at www.uacollegesavings.com or by phone at
866-277-1005

Arizona
Maximum investment: $187,000
Minimum investment: $50 per pay period with direct deposits;
$25 per pay period for large institutions
Contact: Online at http://arizona.collegesavings.com or by phone
at 800-888-2723

Arkansas
Maximum investment: $245,000
Minimum investment: $250 lump sum for residents; $1,000 lump
sum for nonresidents
Contact: Online at www.thegiftplan.com or by phone at
877-442-6553

California
Maximum investment: Between $124,799 and $174,648, depending on the age of the beneficiary
Minimum investment: $15 per pay period
Contact: Online at www.scholarshare.com or by phone at
877-728-4338

Colorado
Maximum investment: $235,000
Minimum investment: $25
Contact: Online at www.scholars-choice.com or by phone at
800-478-5651 (in-state) or 888-572-4652 (out of state)

Connecticut
Maximum investment: $235,000
Minimum investment: $25 or $15 per pay period
Contact: Online at www.aboutchet.com or by phone at
888-799-CHET (888-799-2438)

Delaware
Maximum investment: $250,000
Minimum investment: $500
Contact: Online at www.fidelity.com/delaware or by phone at
800-544-1655

Florida
Maximum investment: $283,000
Minimum investment: $25
Contact: Online at www.florida529plans.com or by phone at
800-552-GRAD (800-552-4723)

Georgia
Maximum investment: $235,000
Minimum investment: $15 through automatic deposits
Contact: Online at www.gacollegesavings.com or by phone at
877-424-4377

Hawaii
Maximum investment: $253,000
Minimum investment: $15
Contact: Online at www.tuitionedge.com or by phone at
866-529-3343

Idaho
Maximum investment: $235,000
Minimum investment: $15 per pay period with automatic deposits
Contact: Online at www.idsaves.org or by phone at 866-433-2533

Illinois
Maximum investment: $235,000
Minimum investment: $25 initially; subsequently, $15
Contact: Online at www.brightstartsavings.com or by phone at
877-432-7444

Indiana
Maximum investment: $236,750
Minimum investment: $50 initially; subsequently, $25
Contact: Online at www.collegechoiceplan.com or by phone at
866-400-7526

Iowa
Maximum investment: $146,000
Minimum investment: $50
Contact: Online at www.collegesavingsiowa.com or by phone at
888-672-9116

Kansas
Maximum investment: $235,000
Minimum investment: $25 a month for in-state residents; $50 a
month for out-of-state residents
Contact: Online at www.learningquestsavings.com or by phone at
800-579-2203

Kentucky
Maximum investment: $235,000
Minimum investment: $15 per pay period through automatic deposits
Contact: Online at www.kentuckytrust.org or by phone at
877-598-7878

Louisiana
Maximum investment: $173,065
Minimum investment: $10
Contact: Online at www.osfa.state.la.us/START.htm or by phone
at 800-259-5626, ext. 1012

Maine
Maximum investment: $235,000
Minimum investment: $50 per month through automatic deposits
Contact: Online at www.nextgenplan.com or by phone at
877-463-9843

Maryland
Maximum investment: $250,000
Minimum investment: $25 per month through automatic deposits
Contact: Online at www.collegesavingsmd.org or by phone at
888-463-4723

Massachusetts
Maximum investment: $230,000
Minimum investment: $50 per month through automatic deposits
Contact: Online at www.mefa.org or by phone at 800-544-2776

Michigan
Maximum investment: $235,000
Minimum investment: $15 per pay period through automatic deposits
Contact: Online at www.misaves.com or by phone at
877-861-6377

Minnesota

Maximum investment: $235,000
Minimum investment: $15 through automatic payroll deposits
Contact: Online at www.mnsaves.org or by phone at
877-338-4646

Mississippi

Maximum investment: $235,000
Minimum investment: $15 through automatic payroll deposits
Contact: Online at www.collegesavingsms.com or by phone at
800-486-3670

Missouri

Maximum investment: $235,000
Minimum investment: $15 through automatic payroll deposits
Contact: Online at www.missourimost.org or by phone at
888-414-6678

Montana

Maximum investment: $187,000
Minimum investment: $25 through automatic payroll deposits
Contact: Online at http://montana.collegesavings.com or by phone
at 800-888-2723

Nebraska

Maximum investment: $250,000
Minimum investment:
AIM: $50 for automatic deposits
College Savings Plan of Nebraska: No minimum
TD Waterhouse: $10 through payroll deductions
Contact: AIM: www.aimfunds.com (877-246-7526); College
Savings Plan of Nebraska: www.planforcollegenow.com
(888-993-3746); TD Waterhouse: www.tdwaterhouse.com
(877-408-4644)

Nevada
Maximum investment: $250,000
Minimum investment: $50 with automatic deposits
Contact: American Skandia College Savings Program:
www.americanskandia.com (800-752-6342);
Strong Capital: www.strong529plan.com (877-529-5295)

New Hampshire
Maximum investment: $233,240
Minimum investment: $50 for automatic deposits
Contact: Online at www.fidelity.com/unique or by phone at
800-544-1722

New Jersey
Maximum investment: $185,000
Minimum investment: $25 per month
Contact: Online at www.hesaa.org/students/njbest or by phone at
877-465-2378

New Mexico
Maximum investment: $294,000
Minimum investment: $25 per month through automatic deposits
Contact: Arrive Education Savings Plan: www.arrive529.com
(877-277-4838); CollegeSense 529 Higher Education
Savings Plan: www.collegesense.com (866-529-
7367); Education Plan's College Savings Program:
www.theeducationplan.com (877-337-5268); Scholar's
Edge: www.scholarsedge529.com (866-529-7283);

New York
Maximum investment: $235,000
Minimum investment: $15 per pay period
Contact: Online at www.nysaves.com or by phone at
877-697-2837

North Carolina
Maximum investment: $268,804
Minimum investment:
NC National: $5
Seligman College Horizon: $100 per month through payroll deductions
Contact: NC National: www.cfnc.org/savings (800-600-3453);
Seligman College Horizon: www.seligman529.com
(800-221-2783)

North Dakota
Maximum investment: $269,000
Minimum investment: $25 per month
Contact: Online at www.collegesave4u.com or by phone at
866-728-3529

Ohio
Maximum investment: $232,000
Minimum investment: $15 for Ohio residents; $15 per month through automatic deposits for everyone else.
Contact: Ohio College Advantage: www.collegeadvantage.com
(800-233-6734); Putnam College Advantage: www.putna
minvestments.com (800-225-1581)

Oklahoma
Maximum investment: $235,000
Minimum investment: $15 per pay period through automatic deposits
Contact: Online at www.ok4saving.org or by phone at
877-654-7284

Oregon
Maximum investment: $250,000
Minimum investment: $25 per month through automatic deposits
Contact: Online at www.oregoncollegesavings.com or by phone at
866-772-8464

Pennsylvania
Maximum investment: $290,000
Minimum investment: $25 for the guaranteed fund; $50 for other investment choices
Contact: Online at www.tap529.com or by phone at 800-440-4000

Rhode Island
Maximum investment: $287,070
Minimum investment: $1,000 or $50 a month. (Lower minimums for in-state residents)
Contact: Online at www.collegeboundfund.com or by phone at 888-324-5057

South Carolina
Maximum investment: $250,000
Minimum investment: None if deposits are made through payroll deductions
Contact: Online at www.futurescholar.com or by phone at 800-765-2668

South Dakota
Maximum investment: $305,000
Minimum investment: $50 per month through automatic deposits
Contact: Online at www.collegeaccess529.com or by phone at 866-529-7462

Tennessee
Maximum investment: $235,000
Minimum investment: $15 per pay period
Contact: Online at www.tnbest.com or by phone at 888-486-2378

Texas
Maximum investment: $257,460
Minimum investment: $15 through automatic deposits
Contact: Online at www.enterprise529.com or by phone at 800-445-4723

Utah
Maximum investment: $260,000
Minimum investment: $25 with automatic deposits
Contact: Online at www.uesp.org or by phone at 800-418-2551

Vermont
Maximum investment: $240,100
Minimum investment: $15 per pay period through automatic deposits
Contact: Online at www.vsac.org or by phone at 800-637-5860

Virginia
Virginia has two 529 plans and a pre-paid education program,
all of which can be reached through the state's website at
www.virginia529.com
Maximum investment: $250,000
Minimum investment: $25 a month; at least $250 by the end of the
first year
Contact: Online at www.virginia529.com or by phone at
888-567-0540 or 800-421-4120 (for CollegeAmerica)

Washington
Maximum investment: $26,000 (for 500 units)
Minimum investment: $20 per month by payroll deduction for
lump sum plan
Contact: Online at www.get.wa.gov or by phone at 877-438-8848

Washington, D.C.
Maximum investment: $260,000
Minimum investment: $15 through payroll deduction
Contact: Online at www.dc529.com or by phone at
800-987-4859

West Virginia
Maximum investment: $265,620
Minimum investment: $15 per month (in-state residents); $50 per
month (out-of-state residents)
Contact: Online at www.smart529.com or by phone at 866-574-3542

Wisconsin
Maximum investment: $246,000
Minimum investment: $25 per month through automatic deposits
Contact: EdVest: www.edvest.com (888-338-3789); Tomorrow's
    Scholar: http://tomorrowsscholar.com (866-677-6933)

Wyoming
Maximum investment: $245,000
Minimum investment: $250 for Wyoming residents; $1,000 for
everyone else
Contact: Online at www.collegeachievementplan.com or by phone
    at 877-529-2655

College Costs and General Information

The two definitive sources of college information both originate from the College Board. This organization processes student-aid applications; formulates aptitude tests; and does frequent, comprehensive studies on the cost of college. If you have Web access, point your browser to www.collegeboard.com. The left side of the screen allows you to plug in the name of any college your child is considering and learn virtually every relevant detail about the school's programs, from athletics to academics. The current-year cost of tuition, books, room and board, and other fees is also included, along with contact information for the college. Websites don't get better than this.

If you don't have Web access, head to the bookstore for the *The College Board College Cost & Financial Aid Handbook* (College Board, 2003; $22.95) The financial-aid section of this book is cursory. The purpose of buying it is for the comprehensive listing of 2,700 four- and two-year colleges, replete with contact information, costs, and scholarship information.

Federal Aid

For questions and general information about federal financial aid options, call 800-4-FED-AID (800-433-3243) or visit the Department of Education's website at www.ed.gov.

To fill out the Free Application for Federal Financial Aid online, visit www.fafsa.ed.gov. You can print the forms or fill them out online. But if you want to use the online application process, you'll need to first visit www.pin.ed.gov to get a personal identification number.

For one of the best nongovernment financial aid sites, go to www.finaid.org. It's also got a link to a site called "FastWeb," which helps students search for private scholarships.

Financial Aid

State education departments keep information on education programs and student aid available through the state. Here are the phone numbers for all the state education departments.

Alabama:	334-242-1998
Alaska:	800-441-2962
Arizona:	602-229-2591
Arkansas:	800-547-8839
California:	916-526-8047
Colorado:	303-866-2723
Connecticut:	860-947-1833
Delaware:	800-292-7935
District of Columbia:	202-698-2400
Florida:	888-827-2004
Georgia:	800-766-6878
Hawaii:	808-956-8213
Idaho:	208-334-2270
Illinois:	800-899-4722

Indiana:	317-232-2350
Iowa:	800-383-4222
Kansas:	785-296-3421
Kentucky:	800-928-8926
Louisiana:	800-259-5626
Maine:	800-228-3734
Maryland:	410-260-4565
Massachusetts:	617-994-6950
Michigan:	877-323-2287
Minnesota:	800-657-0866
Mississippi:	601-432-6997
Missouri:	800-473-6757
Montana:	800-537-7508
Nebraska:	402-471-2847
Nevada:	702-486-7330
New Hampshire:	603-271-2555
New Jersey:	800-792-8670
New Mexico:	800-279-9777
New York:	888-697-4372
North Carolina:	919-549-8614
North Dakota:	701-328-4114
Ohio:	888-833-1133
Oklahoma:	800-858-1840
Oregon:	800-452-8807
Pennsylvania:	800-692-7392
Rhode Island:	800-922-9855
South Carolina:	803-737-2260
South Dakota:	605-773-3455
Tennessee:	615-741-3605
Texas:	800-242-3062
Utah:	800-418-8757
Vermont:	800-642-3177
Virginia:	804-225-2600
Washington:	360-753-7800
West Virginia:	888-825-5707
Wisconsin:	608-267-2206
Wyoming:	307-777-7763

Individual Development Accounts

If you are a low-income worker who wants to go back to school, check into IDA programs at www.idanetwork.org. If you're lucky, you'll find a nearby program that will be willing to match your savings dollar-for-dollar—or better—if you use that savings for one of the plan's handful of qualified goals.

Investment Information

To help compare fees charged by 529 plans or mutual funds that have disparate fee structures, go to www.sec.gov. Click on Investor Information, then on Interactive Tools, and finally on Mutual Fund Cost Calculator.

For a primer on buying and selling individual stocks, check out my book *Investing 101* (Bloomberg Press, 2000; $15.95). Also, on the Web you can. go to www.latimes.com. Click on Business and Times University to find a somewhat more abbreviated investing series.

Loyalty Buying Programs

Hey, big spender. Here are three websites to check out, if you think you might want to spend yourself—or a child, relative, or friend—to college wealth:
- ❑ www.babymint.com
- ❑ www.edexpress.com
- ❑ www.upromise.com

252

Tuition Rewards Colleges in the BabyMint Plan

If you are a member of the BabyMint loyalty buying program, you'll need to know which colleges participate in the company's tuition rewards program. These colleges agree to match a student's BabyMint savings on a dollar-for-dollar basis, through college scholarships and tuition discounts. These are the schools that currently participate in the program, in alphabetical order, by state and college:

California
Concordia University
United States International University
University of La Verne
Westmont College
Whittier College

Connecticut
University of Bridgeport

Delaware
Wesley College

Florida
Florida Southern College

Georgia
Shorter College

Illinois
Augustana College
Barat College
DePaul University
Dominican University

Greenville College
Judson College
Lake Forest College
McKendree College
North Park University
Robert Morris College
St. Xavier University

Indiana

Marian College
Tri-State University

Iowa

Briar Cliff College
Buena Vista University
Coe College
Iowa Wesleyan College
Loras College
Morningside College
St. Ambrose University

Kansas

Benedictine College

Kentucky

Campbellsville University
Georgetown College
Lindsey Wilson College

Maine

St. Joseph's College

Maryland

Capital Bible Seminary
Washington Bible College

Massachusetts
Clark University

Michigan
Adrian College
Alma College
Aquinas College
Hillsdale College
Olivet College
University of Detroit Mercy

Minnesota
Augsburg College
College of St. Scholastica
Concordia College-Moorhead
Concordia University-St. Paul
St. Mary's University

Missouri
Avila College
Kansas City Art Institute
William Jewell College

Nebraska
Hastings College
Midland Lutheran College
York College

New Jersey
Fairleigh Dickinson University
Felician College
Georgian Court College

New York
Alfred University
College of New Rochelle

College of Saint Rose
Elmira College
Hilbert College
Manhattanville College
Marymount College
Medaille College
Pratt Institute
Roberts Wesleyan College
St. Lawrence University
St. Thomas Aquinas College
Wagner College

North Carolina
Catawba College
Chowan College
Less-McRae College
Montreat College
Mount Olive College
Pfeiffer College
St. Andrews Presbyterian College

Ohio
Antioch University
Ashland University
Baldwin-Wallace College
Lake Erie College
Ohio Wesleyan University
Otterbein College
Tiffin University
University of Findlay
Ursuline College
Wilberforce University
Wilmington College

Pennsylvania
Albright College

Allegheny College
Arcadia University
Cedar Crest College
College Misericordia
Delaware Valley College
De Sales University
Drexel University
Duquesne University
Eastern College
Gannon University
Geneva College
Gwynedd Mercy College
Holy Family College
Immaculata College
Keystone College
Kings College
Marywood University
Mercyhurst College
Moore College of Art and Design
Mount Aloysius College
Point Park College
Rosemont College
St. Francis College
St. Vincent College
Seton Hill College
Thiel College
Washington and Jefferson College
Westminster College
Widener University
Wilkes University
Wilson College

South Carolina
Coker College
Limestone College

South Dakota
Augustana College

Tennessee
Crichton College
Cumberland University
Lincoln Memorial University

Texas
Schreiner University

Virginia
Bridgewater College
Ferrum College
Liberty University
Randolph-Macon College
Virginia Intermont College

West Virginia
Bethany College
Davis and Elkins College
Salem-Teikyo University
Wheeling Jesuit University

Wisconsin
Alverno College
Carroll College
Lawrence University
Marian College of Fond du Lac
Mount Mary College
Milwaukee Institute of Art & Design
Ripon College
St. Norbert College

Savings Bonds

Information on U.S. government savings bonds, one of the all-time most popular investments for college, can be found at www.savingsbonds.gov.

Index

About Bloomberg

Bloomberg L.P., founded in 1981, is a global information services, news, and media company. Headquartered in New York, the company has nine sales offices, two data centers, and 87 news bureaus worldwide.

Bloomberg, serving customers in 126 countries around the world, holds a unique position within the financial services industry by providing an unparalleled range of features in a single package, the BLOOMBERG PROFESSIONAL® service. By addressing the demand for investment performance and efficiency through an exceptional combination of information, analytic, electronic trading, and Straight Through Processing tools, Bloomberg has built a worldwide customer base of corporations, issuers, financial intermediaries, and institutional investors.

BLOOMBERG NEWS®, founded in 1990, provides stories and columns on business, general news, politics, and sports to leading newspapers and magazines throughout the world. BLOOMBERG TELEVISION®, a 24-hour business and financial news network, is produced and distributed globally in seven different languages. BLOOMBERG RADIO^{SM} is an international radio network anchored by flagship station BLOOMBERG® 1130 (WBBR-AM) in New York.

In addition to the BLOOMBERG PRESS® line of books, Bloomberg publishes *BLOOMBERG MARKETS*™ and *BLOOMBERG WEALTH MANAGER®*. To learn more about Bloomberg, call a sales representative at:

Frankfurt:	49-69-92041-280	São Paulo:	5511-3048-4506
Hong Kong:	852-2977-6900	Singapore:	65-6212-1100
London:	44-20-7330-7500	Sydney:	612-9777-8686
New York:	1-212-318-2200	Tokyo:	813-3201-8910
San Francisco:	1-415-912-2970		

About the Author

Kathy Kristof, author of *Investing 101* (Bloomberg Press, 2000), is a syndicated financial columnist for Tribune Media Services, Her columns reach 40 million people in more than fifty major newspapers nationwide, including the *Los Angeles Times,* the *Chicago Tribune,* the *Philadelphia Inquirer,* the *Dallas Morning News,* and New York's *Daily News.* She joined the *Los Angeles Times* in 1989 to write about banking, insurance, and the securities industry. In 1990 Kristof began writing a personal finance column for the *Times* and was named to replace syndicated personal finance journalist Sylvia Porter, when Porter died in 1991. Esteemed by her journalist peers (cited as "maybe the best reporter of all the personal finance columnists" in the prestigious TJFR 1999 Blue Chip Newsroom ranking of the top 100 American business journalists), she has received numerous writing awards and honors, including a John Hancock award for news reporting, an ICI/American University excellence in personal finance reporting award, and the Consumer Advocate of the Year award in 1998 from the California Alliance for Consumer Education. Kristof serves as president of the Society of American Business Editors and Writers. In addition to writing, she is a frequent lecturer at investment conferences. She also appears regularly on radio and television news programs, including CNN, CNBC, and *Nightly Business Report.* She lives in southern California with her two children.

FOR IN-DEPTH MARKET INFORMATION AND NEWS, visit the Bloomberg website at **www.bloomberg.com,** which draws from the news and power of the BLOOMBERG PROFESSIONAL® service and Bloomberg's host of media products to provide high-quality news and information in multiple languages on stocks, bonds, currencies, and commodities.